I0759805

THE GREATEST STAR

11454-95

THE GREATEST STAR

Behind the Scenes of *Sunset Boulevard*

The Official 75th Anniversary
Collector's Edition

Jeffrey Vance

Foreword by Nancy Olson Livingston

weldon**owen**

Gloria Swanson
Erich von Stroheim
William Holden
Sunset Boulevard
Produced by B. Wilder
Paramount Picture

CONTENTS

Foreword

By Nancy Olson Livingston

In the 1930s, '40s, and '50s, Paramount Pictures was one of the biggest studios in Hollywood, producing motion pictures for theaters they owned around the world. It had under contract big-name producers and directors like Cecil B. DeMille, William Wyler, Hal Wallis, and Billy Wilder; writers, composers, art directors, wardrobe creators, hair dressers, and makeup artists; and assistant directors putting all the technical workers in place. And they were all working every day for a single employer.

Around the time that *Sunset Boulevard* was made, Paramount also had under contract actors and actresses like Bing Crosby, Bob Hope, Alan Ladd, Veronica Lake, Betty Hutton, Dean Martin, Jerry Lewis, and many more—including me.

Back then, stars were a studio's most prized commodity. The public didn't care if a picture was produced by a well-known director; it was all about the names above the title. So the studios made these popular performers larger than life, larger than any other human beings in the world—more beautiful, more sexual, more interesting, more beguiling; they made them legends. And the stars didn't just cooperate, they projected as much as they could of their specialness, to the exclusion of almost everything else in their lives, to stay on top.

But when they entered their thirties and forties, they no longer had the advantage of youth to maintain that illustrious veneer. So after years of being led to believe they were the greatest, most captivating people in the world, the studios just threw them away. And it always seemed that it was the biggest stars who were the most vulnerable to this tragedy.

When I was contracted to Paramount Studios in 1948, I learned all of this firsthand, very early on. In all my time making movies, I never met an actor or actress who had a successful family life. I saw how stardom was an impossible demand on the human psyche and an endless pursuit of something that could never truly be achieved.

When I was cast as Betty Schaefer, I read the script for *Sunset Boulevard* and immediately understood that this was a story like no other. It was a daring and brutally honest portrayal of an iconic star's life gone tragically and horribly wrong, but had at its heart a story of discarding stars that was as old as the studio system itself. Unbeknownst to me, it would just so happen to be a foreshadowing of what would ultimately lead me to leave the industry after what was a relatively short career.

When I heard that Gloria Swanson was going to play Norma Desmond, I had no idea who she was. It was my mother who filled me in about her great stardom in the 1920s. Mae West had apparently been the first choice to play Norma; thank God she refused. The film could have slid dangerously toward the cliff of high camp if anybody, particularly in the Norma Desmond role, had gone overboard. Gloria was the inspired choice, and so was William Holden. They originally wanted Montgomery Clift to play the role of Joe Gillis, but he also refused. The film would never have been what it is if Gloria and Bill had not played these two parts.

Bill Holden's first two legendary classic films, *Golden Boy* (1939) and *Our Town* (1940), were the beginning of a great career, but these successes were interrupted by the war. Bill was drafted into the army. When he came back to the studio, his career was increasingly fragmented with undistinguished and irrelevant roles. He was in a marriage that was falling apart. He was drinking too much. And he was beginning to feel desperate. Bill brought all of that, all that was going on in his life, into the role of Joe—a man who was also desperate, who sold his soul for survival. Erich von Stroheim as Max was inspired casting as well. Erich was once a promising director, like his character, and he understood on a deep level the ephemeral nature of being a commodity in Hollywood. Together, the cast was the perfect combination of sensibilities to bring these characters to life, with a common theme that each, in their own way, was an opportunist.

I met Billy Wilder walking to and from the commissary on the Paramount lot prior to making *Sunset Boulevard*. He would pepper me with questions about my life growing up in the Midwest. I think he saw my wholesome upbringing as the perfect counterpoint to the sad and sordid relationship taking place between Joe and Norma on the fringes of the film industry.

The buzz about the picture started long before the film was ever finished. At Paramount Pictures there were approximately twelve movies being filmed on the lot every day. There was a small theater that showed the dailies. The footage that was shot the day before was shown the next evening at 6 p.m. to the director, the cameraman, and to the writers. Everyone came to see their own work, and of course sometimes they saw other films that had been shot the day before as they waited for their own footage to appear onscreen. As soon as the dailies for *Sunset Boulevard* began to run, there was an intense interest and curiosity about what was coming next. The studio had to put in extra chairs, because people would not leave until the *Sunset Boulevard* scenes were screened.

When *Sunset Boulevard* opened in New York, *The New York Times*, the *Herald Tribune*, the *New York Post*, and every other publication across the country wrote that this film was one of the most compelling and perhaps one of the greatest ever made.

Over the years, I have often reflected on just what it was that made *Sunset Boulevard* stand out the way it did. What is the secret ingredient that creates a masterpiece? Certainly there have been films over the years that have risen to the status of timeless works of art, films that are still playing every day all over the world, like *Gone with the Wind*, *The Wizard of Oz*, *The Godfather*, *It's a Wonderful Life*, and *Sunset Boulevard*. What is it that makes these movies so special?

As best as I can describe it, a work of great art reveals the truth.

When *Sunset Boulevard* was first screened for the major executives in the film industry, Louis B. Mayer walked over to Billy Wilder after the screening and said, "How could you do this to us?"

Billy answered. "Go fuck yourself," and walked out.

I think that pretty much sums it up. The truth is not always popular, but in the end, it stands the test of time. And *Sunset Boulevard* is as relevant today as it was the day it first premiered.

Norma Desmond says, "Stars are ageless." But in reality, it's the truth that endures. And if that is the case, *Sunset Boulevard* will always be on the list of the greatest films ever made.

—NANCY OLSON LIVINGSTON

Sunset Boulevard

Billy Wilder's Final Cut on Hollywood

By Jeffrey Vance

"I am big. It's the pictures that got small."

This line of dialogue, written by Charles Brackett and Billy Wilder[1] and spoken by aging silent-movie queen Norma Desmond in Billy Wilder's *Sunset Boulevard,* is as relevant today as it was seventy-five years ago. In 1950, Norma was referring to the popularization of talking films and the growing acceptance of television. Today, Norma could just as easily be referring to streaming services and social media. But one thing is certain: Norma is still big, frequently quoted, and firmly part of mainstream culture. One need look no further than the staging of the recent West End and Broadway revival of Andrew Lloyd Webber's musical *Sunset Blvd.*, based on the film, with its larger-than-life projections of Norma on a screen accompanied by her bravura ballads. *Sunset Boulevard* was among the initial group of films selected for the National Film Registry in 1989. It is regularly placed on any serious list of the finest films ever made. As the film celebrates another milestone anniversary, it offers a perfect excuse to revisit Wilder's masterpiece and the Hollywood era it captures.

In 1948, the refined and celebrated screenwriting team of Charles Brackett and Billy Wilder was contemplating a story idea that would draw on Hollywood's past. The seminal idea and tone crystallized with the ignominious death of pioneering film director D. W. Griffith in July of that year. (Brackett, in his diaries, describes Griffith as "one of the first and loathsome victims of Hollywooditis," a derogatory term for the sickness of fleeting fame that characterizes the business of filmmaking.)[2] Brackett gave the eulogy for "the father of film," who was struck down by a cerebral hemorrhage in the lobby of the Knickerbocker Hotel, located off Hollywood Boulevard in Hollywood, years after being discarded by the town he helped to create. (Erich von Stroheim, who plays Max Von Mayerling in *Sunset Boulevard,*

above: D. W. Griffith, looking at a wall of his past triumphs, c. 1948.

remarked that Griffith died "in the heart of the most heartless town in the world."[3])

In addition, by the late 1940s, the perception of Hollywood—and the Hollywood studio system—was crumbling as a result of the Paramount Decree (a series of consent decrees issued in 1948 by the US Supreme Court that forced the major motion picture studios to sell their theaters to avoid violations of antitrust laws), the Hollywood blacklist, and the advent and popularity of television. David O. Selznick, the maverick producer of *Gone with the Wind* (1939), believed the parade had gone by as early as 1951. "Hollywood's like Egypt," Selznick told screenwriter Ben Hecht. "Full of crumbled pyramids. It'll never come back. It'll just keep on crumbling until finally the wind blows the last studio prop across the sands."[4]

It was this context in which Wilder and Brackett began to develop their Hollywood tale of a fading silent-film star who keeps a hungry young writer as her codependent collaborator and lover. Hollywood has a long history of self-referential films; the finest prior to *Sunset Boulevard* is unquestionably William A.

Wellman's *A Star is Born* (1937), which, like *Sunset Boulevard,* features a brilliant screenplay. (Both films won Academy Awards for their screenplays. Produced by David O. Selznick at the height of the Golden Age of Hollywood, *A Star is Born* is more forgiving of the motion picture industry. But this was a different era, and their movie was going to reflect it. *Sunset Boulevard* was going to be an uncompromising indictment of Hollywood, brilliantly blurring fact and fiction. Indeed, Brackett and Wilder went into production without a completed script and with the deliberately vague working title *A Can of Beans.* They were wary of being prevented from making a film that, in effect, bites the hand that feeds them.

MAE WEST WAS their initial choice for Norma, when the material was more in a comedic vein. West, however, was a great personality rather than a fine dramatic actress. She was cast aside, and Gloria Swanson became their ideal Norma. (Although Brackett and Wilder met with legendary silent-film star and producer Mary Pickford at Pickfair, this may have been to provide some grist for their creative mill rather than offering the passé Pickford the role.) Montgomery Clift was the original choice for the role of the gigolo and actually accepted the part. However, he withdrew at the last moment, possibly because the subject matter was too close for comfort given his current May–December relationship

below: The Normas that might have been: Mae West (left) and Mary Pickford, c. 1950.

with forty-eight-year-old socialite and actress Libby Holman. The part ultimately went to William Holden, cementing his place in Hollywood history and an association with Wilder that spanned nearly thirty years and included *Stalag 17* (1953)—for which Holden won the Academy Award for Best Actor—*Sabrina* (1954), and *Fedora* (1978), a strange tale of a reclusive film star that has striking similarities to *Sunset Boulevard.*

The film's greatness is in no small measure due to the brilliant and inspired casting of silent-film era notables, which imbued the film with credibility. Casting Gloria Swanson, a silent-screen legend whose own star was on the edge of obscurity, had a significant effect in making the part of Norma Desmond more sympathetic and believable. Former silent-film director Erich von Stroheim plays former silent-film director Max Von Mayerling. At one point in the film, Max projects at Norma's home the film Stroheim directed for Swanson in 1928–1929—the abandoned *Queen Kelly,* which effectively ended the profligate Stroheim's career as a director. Filmmaker (and a founding father of Hollywood) Cecil B. DeMille—who had made Swanson a major star—and notorious gossip columnist Hedda Hopper play themselves. Cameo appearances by silent-screen stars Buster Keaton, Anna Q. Nilsson, and H. B. Warner as the so-called waxworks who make up Norma's regular bridge game also give the film great

opposite: Gloria Swanson in a promotional photo for *Queen Kelly*, c. 1928.
above: Gloria Swanson first imitated Chaplin's Little Tramp character on film in Allan Dwan's *Manhandled* (1924). The film survives, but the sequence does not.

above: Gloria with the former silent-film stars who made up the "waxworks" in *Sunset Boulevard*: (left to right) Buster Keaton, Anna Q. Nilsson, and H. B. Warner.
opposite: Jay Livingston and Ray Evans in the party sequence at Artie's apartment.

authenticity. So, too, are filming locations that exist to this day: the Chateau Alto Nido Apartments, Bel-Air Country Club golf course, Paramount Pictures' instantly recognizable Bronson Gate, and the distinctive Washington Square set (built for William Wyler's 1949 film *The Heiress*) on the Paramount backlot.

The film originally opened and closed with scenes set in the County of Los Angeles Medical Examiner and Morgue facility. The morgue scenes were unintentionally amusing to a preview audience and were cut in favor of the film's inspired opening, which begins with a shot of the street that gave the film its name, Sunset Blvd. Rather than depicting swaying palm trees or beams of sunshine warming the roadway, instead Wilder shows the viewer the name of the boulevard stenciled onto the gutter, a harbinger of the tale to come. After a race to the rescue to a dilapidated Beverly Hills mansion (race to the rescues were a staple of the early silent movies), the film's protagonist is found dead, floating in the swimming pool—the ultimate Hollywood status symbol. The film's story is told by the deceased man in the form of a flashback. Another sequence, cut before the film's release, features the singing of"The Paramount-Don't-Want-Me Blues" at the New Year's Eve party given by Artie Green

(Jack Webb) and his girlfriend Betty Schaefer (Nancy Olson). Although the morgue footage does not survive, "The Paramount-Don't-Want-Me Blues" footage survives as a fully cut sequence lifted from the film shortly before release. It is a delight to watch.

I AM A FILM HISTORIAN specializing in silent cinema, and *Sunset Boulevard* has been a favorite of mine for more than forty years. I first experienced the film when I was just ten and the film only thirty. Revivals of *Sunset Boulevard* were frequent at the time, with the publication of Swanson's best-selling autobiography, *Swanson on Swanson*, in 1980. I was fortunate enough to meet Ms. Swanson and stare into her enormous blue eyes. Her steely glare—visible under her bolero hat—turned to an affectionate gaze when I was able to discuss two-reelers she made back in 1915. She twirled the red carnation in her hand with delight and cheerfully answered my questions while reminding me she lived in the present and was nothing like the character of Norma Desmond. Additionally, I attended a New Year's Eve party where songwriter Ray Evans pounded out "Buttons and Bows" on an upright piano (echoes of Artie Green's New Year's Eve

opposite: Billy Wilder with his star.

party) while he and Jay Livingston sang it, their Oscar-winning song. I also briefly was a bridge partner to Mrs. Buster Keaton, the wife of one of the film's waxworks. For me, these encounters solidified the authenticity of Wilder's film. Sadly, *Sunset Boulevard*'s remarkable cast of characters are nearly all gone. Only Nancy Olson (ninety-seven years of age at the time of this writing) remains. I have had the privilege to spend time in her company. She occasionally attends screenings of *Sunset Boulevard* and regales audiences with her vivid recollections, astute observations, and enduring glamour.[5]

One of the most exhilarating afternoons of my life was spent having lunch with Billy Wilder in Beverly Hills thirty years ago, where we discussed silent films in general and *Sunset Boulevard* in particular. Wilder grew up with silent films. For Wilder, Charles Chaplin (when he was silent, at least) was a god, and Greta Garbo was a deity. As a nod to the silent era and a reminder of the stars who once ruled Hollywood, Wilder included Norma doing a memorable imitation of Chaplin's Little Tramp character and had her reference Garbo as the only living star she acknowledges as a peer.

Wilder was a sardonic observer and a superb storyteller. "Everything just fell into my lap," he remembered of *Sunset Boulevard*.[6] "I wanted Swanson. I got Swanson. I wanted someone who knew silent pictures. I got cameraman John Seitz. He shot Rudolph Valentino dancing the tango in the silent days. I wanted DeMille; I got Cecil B. DeMille. He was making *Samson and Delilah* (1949) on the Paramount lot. I needed the Paramount lot. I got the Paramount lot. I needed a great face. I got Buster Keaton. I was lucky." He felt obliged to salute Swanson. "Swanson was perfect. She got it. She knew silent-picture acting. You can't teach somebody how to do that. It was a different technique. It could have been too much and become ridiculous. She never overplayed it. She knew just how far to go."

Without missing a beat, Wilder also remarked, "The pet chimpanzee was Norma's lover. Did you catch that? Bill Holden takes the place of the dead monkey she buried in the garden," just to see my shocked reaction.

Erich von Stroheim was a boyhood idol, with *Foolish Wives* (1922) and *Greed* (1924) being particular Wilder favorites. Stroheim had worked with Wilder previously on *Five Graves to Cairo* (1943). Wilder remembered that when they first met, Wilder clicked his heels and said, "It's an honor to direct you. You were ten years ahead of your time."

"Twenty," was Stroheim's curt reply.

During the production, Wilder listened to Stroheim and often took his suggestions. Stroheim came up with the idea that his character of Max Von Mayerling (Norma Desmond's current butler and chauffeur, former director, and first husband) is the one writing the fan letters to make the delusional Desmond feel like she is still beloved by the public. Wilder also remembered: "Stroheim didn't know how to drive a car. The big Isotta Fraschini car was towed through the Bronson Gate at Paramount."

Wilder recalled the industry-only preview screening of *Sunset Boulevard* on the Paramount studio lot that Metro-Goldwyn-Mayer studio chief Louis B. Mayer attended. The film infuriated Mayer, who believed Wilder's scathing

11454-2/120

above: Erich von Stroheim during the filming of his epic *Greed*, 1924.

indictment of Hollywood was a disgrace to the Hollywood dream-factory culture Mayer himself helped to cultivate. As Mayer began to decry the film—and denigrate Wilder for making it—Wilder interrupted Mayer and directed him to "go shit in [his] hat" and walked away. (There are more colorful variations of this story, like the version Nancy Olson Livingston recalled in her Foreword, but Wilder told me this version.) Perhaps Mayer's criticism struck a nerve not only because Wilder was proud of his film, but also because it was deeply personal to him. Wilder was, at his core, a screenwriter, and *Sunset Boulevard* is essentially Joe Gillis's story, the story of a screenwriter.

Equally amusing (and most likely apocryphal) is the story of silent-film star Mae Murray's reaction to the film; she reportedly commented, "None of us floozies were ever that nuts."[7]

SUNSET BOULEVARD MARKED the culmination and valedictory of the Charles Brackett–Billy Wilder partnership in which the two wrote films together, with Wilder directing and Brackett producing. This collaboration also yielded the classic film *The Lost Weekend* (1945), winner of multiple Oscars, including Best Picture. *Sunset Boulevard*'s superbly constructed screenplay is a masterpiece of storytelling. It weaves together complex characters, sharp dialogue, and a compelling narrative, exploring themes of ambition, delusion, and the dark side of Hollywood.

Sunset Boulevard had its world premiere at Radio City Music Hall in New York City on August 10, 1950, where it enjoyed a profitable run and received excellent reviews. The film brilliantly records a specific time and place, Hollywood after World War II. Apparently, Hollywood—along with the critics and public—agreed with the staging and atmospherics. It was nominated for eleven Academy Awards, including nods for all four stars (Swanson and Holden for Best Actor and Actress, Stroheim and Nancy Olson for Best Supporting Actor and Actress), Billy Wilder for Best Director, and Best Picture. These nominations also acknowledged the film's exceptional artistic and technical achievements, from Franz Waxman's haunting musical score to its evocative settings. *Sunset* won in three categories, for Best Music, Scoring; Best Art Direction–Set Direction, Black-and-White; and Best Writing, Story and Screenplay.

The Hollywood of *Sunset Boulevard* that Norma Desmond and Joe Gillis inhabit is not much different than the Hollywood of today. The lure of fame, either nascent or fleeting, has always drawn opportunists like Norma Desmond and Joe Gillis to Hollywood, people who use others to get ahead—or to crawl back into Hollywood's limelight. And in a town where age often is a box-office curse, there remain the delusions held by the aging, fading stars. As Joe Gillis laments, "Norma, you're a woman of fifty; now grow up. There's nothing tragic about being fifty, not unless you try to be twenty-five." Even the film's title, which references the famous Los Angeles thoroughfare that stretches from downtown to the Pacific Ocean, serves as a metaphor for Norma's journey from stardom to obscurity.

Swanson's performance is one of the greatest ever captured on film. She embodies Norma Desmond with a perfect blend of vulnerability, madness, and faded grandeur, making her a truly unforgettable character and arguably one of the greatest characters ever created by the cinema. "We didn't need dialogue, we had *faces*" is not only authentically voiced by Swanson, there is a level of camp diva grandeur in her singular delivery. Norma Desmond is unforgettable and eternal.

THE FILM'S FINAL SCENE is among the most haunting in cinema. Norma, after murdering Joe Gillis and lost in her delusions, descends her grand staircase acting as a sensual Salome, believing she is making a triumphant return to the screen rather than heading to the ignominious arrest that awaits her. Her once commanding presence is reduced to a tragic spectacle, a stark contrast to the power she wielded in Hollywood's silent era. When she proclaims, "All right, Mr. DeMille, I'm ready for my close-up," it is not just the end of Norma Desmond—it is the end of an era.

Sunset Boulevard remains a film about illusions: the illusions of Hollywood, the illusions of self-importance, and the ultimate illusion of time standing still. The industry moves on, indifferent to its past. But in Norma's eyes—wide, hypnotized, forever searching for the camera and the spotlight—the past never fades. ♦

NOTES

1. The writing team eventually included D. M. Marshman Jr. as well.
2. Quoted in Anthony Slide (editor), *It's the Pictures That Got Small: Charles Brackett on Billy Wilder and Hollywood's Golden Age* (New York: Columbia University Press, 2015), 346.
3. Erich von Stroheim's D. W. Griffith eulogy survives as a 1948 radio broadcast. https://www.youtube.com/watch?v=zdFVO6-35JA&t=4s.
4. David O. Selznick as quoted by Ben Hecht, *A Child of the Century: The Autobiography of Ben Hecht* (New York: Simon and Schuster, 1954), 467.
5. Nancy Olson (as Nancy Olson Livingston) published her autobiography *A Front Row Seat: An Intimate Look at Broadway, Hollywood, and the Age of Glamour* (Lexington: University Press of Kentucky, 2022).
6. Billy Wilder in conversation with Jeffrey Vance, 1995. All subsequent Wilder quotes are from this conversation. Wilder, a master storyteller, often told his Hollywood anecdotes in the same manner. For corroboration, see also David Freeman, "*Sunset Boulevard* Revisited," *The New Yorker* 69, no. 18 (June 21, 1993): 72-79; and Cameron Crowe, *Conversations with Wilder* (New York: Alfred A. Knopf, 1999).
7. Michael G. Ankerich, *Mae Murray: The Girl with the Bee-Stung Lips* (Lexington: University Press of Kentucky, 2013), 279.

opposite: The end of the film—and an era.

THE CHARACTERS

JOE GILLIS................William Holden

NORMA DESMOND............Gloria Swanson

MAX VON MAYERLING........Eric von Stroheim

BETTY SCHAEFER...........Nancy Olson

ARTIE GREEN..............Jack Webb

SHELDRAKE, the producer...

MORINO, the agent.........

A page from the final shooting script. In earlier versions of the character list, under the heading "The Actors We Hope To Get," Montgomery Clift was cast as Dan (not Joe) Gillis, and Betty Schaefer was just listed as "a new face." Max and Norma were always Erich von Stroheim and Gloria Swanson.

PARAMOUNT PICTURES INC.

P.11454

SUNSET BOULEVARD

Charles Brackett
Billy Wilder
D.M. Marshman, Jr.
March 21, 1949

F-23—N-81

Received from Stenographic Dept.

P.11454
March 21, 1949

Title SUNSET BOULEVARD

Signed ____________________

PARAMOUNT PICTURES INC.

SCENE A-1
In both the final shooting script used in this book and the film itself, the opening credit titles are the same. Scenes A-2 through A-6, shown on the following pages, were shot but ultimately scrapped after a disastrous preview screening. (The audience laughed throughout the morgue sequence.) The opening scene of Joe floating in the pool does not appear in this final shooting script.

AJM

SUNSET BOULEVARD

SEQUENCE "A"

A-1 START the picture with the actual street sign: SUNSET BOULEVARD, stencilled on a curbstone. In the gutter lie dead leaves, scraps of paper, burnt matches and cigarette butts. It is early morning.

Now the CAMERA leaves the sign and MOVES EAST, the grey asphalt of the street filling the screen. As speed accelerates to around 40 m.p.h., traffic demarcations, white arrows, speed-limit warnings, manhole covers, etc., flash by. SUPERIMPOSED on all of this are the CREDIT TITLES, in the stencilled style of the street sign.

After the final title, PAN UP to the REAR END OF A MOVING VEHICLE

It is a black County hearse. The license plate says: CALIFORNIA, 1949 -- together with a number. The metal frame around the plate is stamped with the words LOS ANGELES.

PAN UP HIGHER. Painted across the back of the hearse is the word CORONER.

DISSOLVE TO:

A-2 THE CORONER'S HEARSE TURNING DOWN AN ALLEY LEADING INTO THE COUNTY MORGUE

It pulls up before a closed gate of steel grillwork. On the wall is a sign: SOUND HORN. The driver does so. An attendant opens the gate. The hearse passes through it and into

A-3 A TUNNEL, and then into

A-4 A SMALL COURTYARD

The hearse backs up to an unloading platform and again the horn is sounded. Two white-clad attendants come out of the morgue while the driver and a sleepy official descend from the hearse. The attendants open the door in the back of the vehicle and wheel out a hospital cart on which lies a corpse covered with a brownish blanket. Only the corpse's feet show, clad in cheap cotten socks and scuffed moccasins. They are soaking wet. PAN with the feet as the cart is wheeled into a small room near the entrance to the building and brought to a stop.

DISSOLVE TO:

3-19-49

AJM SUNSET BOULEVARD 2.

A-5 SAME ANGLE

The blanket has been replaced by a sheet. The feet are naked. The hands of an attendant come into the shot and attach a linen tag tc the corpse's left big toe. FOCUS ON THE TAG. In ordinary handwriting it reads:

JOSEPH GILLIS
HOMICIDE
5/17/49

DISSOLVE TO:

A-6 THE MORGUE ITSELF

An attendant wheels the dead Gillis into the huge, bare, windowless room. Along the walls are twenty or so sheet-covered corpses lying in an orderly row of wheeled slabs with large numbers painted on the walls above each slab. The attendant pushes Gillis into a vacant space. Beyond him, the feet of the other corpses stretch from under their sheets: men's feet, women's feet, children's, two or three negroes' -- with a linen tag dangling from each left big toe.

The attendant exits, switching off the light. For a moment the room is semi-dark, then as the music takes on a more astral phase, a curious glow emanates from the sheeted corpses. The long row of tags sways in the breeze from the ventilator system.

(NOTE: The voices in the following scene all have a peculiar, hollow quality).

A MAN'S VOICE
Don't be scared. There's a lot of us here. It's all right.

GILLIS
I'm not scared.

His head doesn't move, but his eyes slowly wander to the slab next to him.

There, under a partially transparent sheet, lies a fat man aged 60 or so. His eyes are open, too, and directed at Gillis.

FAT MAN
How did you happen to die?

GILLIS
What difference does it make?

FAT MAN
Died of a heart attack myself. Was

3-19-49

FAT MAN
going to retire right here in L.A. Had a nice pension from the Seattle City Bank and a nice little bungalow all picked out. The agent was just about to show me the avocado tree when it happened.

GILLIS
That's a shame.

FAT MAN
Only lucky thing is, I hadn't signed the lease.

There is a little pause.

GILLIS
Me, I drowned.

On a slab against the opposite wall lies a blond boy of eleven, his swollen, child's face also peering through a transparent sheet.

BOY
So did I. I drowned. Right off the pier at Ocean Park. I bet Pinky Evans I could stay under water longer than two minutes, and I did, too.

Under another sheet lies a husky negro.

NEGRO
You wouldn't know if Satchel Paige beat the White Sox yesterday?

GILLIS
No, I wouldn't. I died before the morning paper came.

NEGRO
Doggone it! I was haulin' some oranges down from San Berdoo, and I just tuned in the baseball scores when she hit me -- crash! Some dame in a Chevvy coupe that was all smashed and stove in and turned turtle. You'da thought I'd be all right in a two-ton truck. Ha, ha! She crawled out and lit herself a cigarette, and me lyin' dead at the crossroads in the middle of all them oranges.

BOY
I wish my folks would come and get me.

Under another sheet lies a middle-aged woman.

WOMAN
They will. Don't worry.

BOY
Do you think they'll be sore at me?

Mc SUNSET BOULEVARD 4.

WOMAN
No, they won't. They'll come for you, and they'll have flowers, and they'll take you someplace where it's sunny and green and tuck you away to lovely dreams.

FAT MAN
Certainly ought to be more life-guards, with all the taxes we pay.
(To Gillis)
Where did you drown? The ocean?

GILLIS
No. Swimming pool.

FAT MAN
A husky fellow like you?

GILLIS
Well, I had a few extra holes in me. Two in the chest, and one in the stomach.

FAT MAN
You were murdered?

GILLIS
Yes, I was murdered.

The fat man's eyes move toward a far corner of the room.

FAT MAN
(Confidentially)
Number seventeen was murdered, too. Interesting man. He was a bookie, he told me. Working for an Eastern syndicate. Only he started taking little bets on his own, so they sent out a couple of men from Chicago. I wonder if the police will ever put that one together.

GILLIS
They'll never put mine together right.
(With the shadow of a wry smile)
It'll be a good joke, lying here like a jigsaw puzzle all scrambled up, with the cops and the Hollywood columnists trying to fit in the wrong pieces.

3-19-49

tv 1st Change SUNSET BOULEVARD 7-18-49 5.

FAT MAN
Hollywood? You in the movies?

GILLIS
Yeah. Came out in forty five, to catch me a swimming pool. And, by gosh, in the end I got myself one. only there turned out to be blood in it.

FAT MAN
Were you an actor?

GILLIS
No. A writer. Never had my name on anything big though. Just a couple of B pictures. One stinker, and the other one -- well, that wasn't so hot either. I was having a tough time making a living.

FAT MAN
It's your dying I was asking about.

Gillis chuckles.

GILLIS
Well, I drove down Sunset Boulevard one afternoon. That was my mistake... Maybe I'd better start off with the morning of that day. I've been out of work for six months...

Gillis' voice overlaps a

SLOW DISSOLVE INTO:

A-7 HOLLYWOOD SEEN FROM THE HILLTOP AT IVAR & FRANKLIN STREETS

In contrast to the eeriness of the morgue, everything is crisp and bright in the sunshine. Gillis' voice continues speaking as the CAMERA PANS toward the ALTO NIDO APARTMENT HOUSE, an ugly stucco Moorish structure, some four stories high. CAMERA MOVES TOWARD AN OPEN WINDOW on the third floor, and right into:

GILLIS' VOICE
I had a couple of stories out that wouldn't sell, and an apartment right above Hollywood and Ivar that wasn't paid for. Come to think of it, a lot of things weren't paid for -- my car, my laundry, Dave the delicatessen man... I was trying to pound out a western this time, but it was like pulling teeth. I was in a slump, all right.

SCENE A-8

A-8 JOE GILLIS' APARTMENT

It is a one-room affair, with an unmade Murphy bed pulled out of the wall. There are a couple of worn-out plush chairs and a Spanish-style, wrought-iron standing lamp. Also a small desk littered with books and letters, and a chest of drawers with a portable phonograph and some records on top. On the walls are a couple of reproductions of characterless paintings, with laundry bills and snapshots stuck in the frames. Through an archway can be seen a tiny kitchenette, complete with unwashed coffee pot and cup, empty tin cans, orange peels, etc. The effect is dingy and cheerless -- just another furnished apartment.

It is about noon. Joe Gillis, barefooted and wearing nothing except shorts and an old bathrobe, is sitting on the bed. In front of him, on a straight chair, is a portable typewriter. Beside him, on the bed, is a dirty ashtray and a scattering of typewritten and pencil-marked pages. Gillis is typing, with a pencil clenched between his teeth.

The buzzer SOUNDS.

GILLIS
Yeah.

The buzzer SOUNDS again. Gillis opens the door. Two men, wearing hats, are standing outside, one of them carrying a briefcase.

NO. 1
Joseph C. Gillis?

GILLIS
That's right.

The men ease into the room. No. 1 hands Gillis a business card.

NO. 1
We've come for the car.

GILLIS
What car?

NO. 2
(Consulting a paper)
1946 Plymouth convertible. California license 97 N 567.

NO. 1
Where are the keys?

GILLIS
Why should I give you the keys?

NO. 1
Because the company's played ball with you long enough. Because you're three payments behind. And because we've got a court order. Come on -- the keys.

NO. 2
Or do you want us to jack it up and haul it away?

GILLIS
Relax, fans. The car isn't here.

NO. 1
Is that so?

GILLIS
I lent it to a friend of mine. He took it up to Palm Springs.

NO. 1
Had to get away for his health, I suppose.

GILLIS
You don't believe me? Look in the garage.

NO. 1
Sure we believe you, only now we want you to believe us. That car better be back here by noon tomorrow, or there's going to be fireworks.

GILLIS
You say the cutest things.

The men leave. Gillis stands pondering beside the door for a moment. Then he walks to the center of the room and, with his back to the CAMERA, slips into a pair of gray slacks. There is a metallic noise as some loose change and keys drop from the trouser pockets. As Gillis bends over to pick them up, we see that he has dropped the car keys, identifiable because of a rabbit's

GILLIS' VOICE
Well, I needed about two hundred and ninety dollars and I needed it real quick, or I'd lose my car. It wasn't in Palm Springs and it wasn't in the garage. I was way ahead of the finance company.

foot and a miniature license plate attached to the key-ring. Gillis pockets the keys and as he starts to put on a shirt

DISSOLVE TO:

A-9 EXTERIOR OF RUDY'S SHOESHINE PARLOR (DAY)

A small shack-like building, it stands in the corner of a public parking lot. Rudy, a colored boy, is giving a customer a shine.

GILLIS' VOICE
(continued)
I knew they'd be coming around and I wasn't taking any chances, so I kept it a couple of blocks away in a parking lot behind Rudy's Shoeshine Parlor. Rudy never asked any questions. He'd just look at your heels and know the score.

PAN BEHIND the shack to GILLIS' CAR, a yellow 1946 Plymouth convertible with the top down. Gillis enters the SHOT. He is wearing a tweed sport jacket, a tan polo shirt, and moccasins. He steps into the car and drives it off. Rudy winks after him.

A-10 THE ALLEY NEXT TO SIDNEY'S MEN'S SHOP ON BRONSON AVE.

Gillis drives into the alley and parks his car right behind a delivery truck. PAN AND FOLLOW HIM as he gets out, walks around the corner into Bronson and then toward the towering main gate of Paramount. A few loafers, studio cops and extras are lounging there.

GILLIS' VOICE
I had an original story kicking around Paramount. My agent told me it was dead as a doornail, but I knew a big shot over there who'd always liked me, and the time had come to take a little advantage of it. His name was Sheldrake. He was a smart producer, with a set of ulcers to prove it.

DISSOLVE TO:

A-11 SHELDRAKE'S OFFICE

It is in the style of a Paramount executive's office--mahogany, leather, and a little chintz. On the walls are some large framed photographs of Paramount stars, with dedications to Mr. Sheldrake. Also a couple of framed critics' awards certificates, and an Oscar on a bookshelf. A shooting schedule chart is thumb-tacked into a large bulletin board. There are

SCENE A-11

Sheldrake: Got a title?
Gillis: Bases Loaded. There's a 40-page outline.

piles of scripts, a few pipes and, somewhere in the background, some set models.

Start on Sheldrake. He is about 45. Behind his worried face there hides a coated tongue. He is engaged in changing the stained filter cigarette in his Zeus holder.

SHELDRAKE
All right, Gillis. You've got five minutes. What's your story about?

GILLIS
It's about a ball player, a rookie shortstop that's batting 347. The poor kid was once mixed up in a hold-up. But he's trying to go straight -- except there's a bunch of gamblers who won't let him.

SHELDRAKE
So they tell the kid to throw the World Series, or else, huh?

GILLIS
More or less. Only for the end I've got a gimmick that's real good.

A secretary enters, carrying a glass of milk. She opens a drawer and takes out a bottle of pills for Sheldrake.

SHELDRAKE
Got a title?

GILLIS
Bases Loaded. There's a 40-page outline.

SHELDRAKE
(To the secretary)
Get the Readers' Department and see what they have on Bases Loaded.

The secretary exits. Sheldrake takes a pill and washes it down with some milk.

GILLIS
They're pretty hot about it over at Twentieth, but I think Zanuck's all wet. Can you see Ty Power as a

GILLIS (cont'd)
shortstop? You've got the best
man for it right here on this lot.
Alan Ladd. Good change of pace for
Alan Ladd. There's another thing:
it's pretty simple to shoot. Lot
of outdoor stuff. Bet you could
make the whole thing for under a
million. And there's a great little
part for Bill Demarest. One of the
trainers, an oldtime player who
got beaned and goes out of his head
sometimes.

The door opens and Betty Schaefer enters -- a clean-cut, nice looking girl of 21, with a bright, alert manner. Dressed in tweed skirt, Brooks sweater and pearls, and carrying a folder of papers. She puts them on Sheldrake's desk, not noticing Gillis, who stands near the door.

BETTY
Hello, Mr. Sheldrake. On that Bases
Loaded. I covered it with a 2-page
synopsis.
(She holds it out)
But I wouldn't bother.

SHELDRAKE
What's wrong with it?

BETTY
It's from hunger.

SHELDRAKE
Nothing for Ladd?

BETTY
Just a rehash of something that
wasn't very good to begin with.

SHELDRAKE
I'm sure you'll be glad to meet
Mr. Gillis. He wrote it.

Betty turns towards Gillis, embarrassed.

SHELDRAKE
This is Miss Kramer.

BETTY
Schaefer. Betty Schaefer. And
right now I wish I could crawl
into a hole and pull it in after
me.

SCENE A-11

Sheldrake: What's wrong with it?
Betty: It's from hunger.
Sheldrake: Nothing for Ladd?
Betty: Just a rehash of something that wasn't very good to begin with.
Sheldrake: I'm sure you'll be glad to meet Mr. Gillis. He wrote it.

GILLIS
If I could be of any help ...

BETTY
I'm sorry, Mr. Gillis, but I just don't think it's any good. I found it flat and banal.

GILLIS
Exactly what kind of material do you recommend? James Joyce? Dostoevsky?

SHELDRAKE
Name dropper.

BETTY
I just think pictures should say a little something.

GILLIS
Oh, you're one of the message kids. Just a story won't do. You'd have turned down Gone With the Wind.

SHELDRAKE
No, that was me. I said, Who wants to see a Civil War picture?

BETTY
Perhaps the reason I hated Bases Loaded is that I knew your name. I'd always heard you had some talent.

GILLIS
That was last year. This year I'm trying to earn a living.

BETTY
So you take Plot 27-A, make it glossy, make it slick --

SHELDRAKE
Careful! Those are dirty words! You sound like a bunch of New York critics. Thank you, Miss Schaefer.

BETTY
Goodbye, Mr. Gillis.

GILLIS
Goodbye. Next time I'll write The Naked and the Dead.

3-19-49

Betty leaves.

SHELDRAKE
Well, seems like Zanuck's got himself a baseball picture.

GILLIS
Mr. Sheldrake, I don't want you to think I thought this was going to win any Academy Award.

SHELDRAKE
(His mind free-wheeling)
Of course, we're always looking for a Betty Hutton. Do you see it as a Betty Hutton?

GILLIS
Frankly, no.

SHELDRAKE
(Amusing himself)
Now wait a minute. If we made it a girls' softball team, put in a few numbers. Might make a cute musical: It Happened in the Bull Pen -- the Story of a Woman.

GILLIS
You trying to be funny? -- because I'm all out of laughs. I'm over a barrel and I need a job.

SHELDRAKE
Sure, Gillis. If something should come along --

GILLIS
Along is no good. I need it now.

SHELDRAKE
Haven't got a thing.

GILLIS
Any kind of assignment. Additional Dialogue.

SHELDRAKE
There's nothing, Gillis. Not even if you were a relative.

GILLIS
(Hating it)
Look, Mr. Sheldrake, could you let me have three hundred bucks yourself, as a personal loan?

SHELDRAKE
Could I? Gillis, last year somebody talked me into buying a ranch in the valley. So I borrowed money from the bank so I could pay for the ranch. This year I had to mortgage the ranch so I could keep up my life insurance so I could borrow on the insurance so I could pay my income tax. Now if Dewey had been elected --

GILLIS
Goodbye, Mr. Sheldrake.

DISSOLVE TO:

A-12 EXT. SCHWAB'S DRUG STORE (EARLY AFTERNOON ACTIVITY)

MOVE IN toward drug store and

DISSOLVE TO:

GILLIS' VOICE
After that I drove down to headquarters. That's the way a lot of us think about Schwab's Drug Store. Actors and stock girls and writers. Kind of a combination office, Kaffee-Klatsch and waiting room. Waiting, waiting for the gravy train.

A-13 INT. SCHWAB'S DRUG STORE

The usual Schwabadero crowd sits at the fountain, gossips at the cigar-stand, loiters by the magazine display. MOVE IN towards the TWO TELEPHONE BOOTHS. In one of them sits Gillis, a stack of nickels in front of him. He's doing a lot of talking into the telephone, hanging up, dropping another nickel, dialing, talking again.

I got myself ten nickels and started sending out a general S.O.S. Couldn't get hold of my agent, naturally. So then I called a pal of mine, name of Artie Green -- an awful nice guy, an assistant director. He could let me have twenty, but twenty wouldn't do.

11454-1

VW 2nd Change SUNSET BOULEVARD 7-18-49 14.

GILLIS' VOICE (Cont'd)
Then I talked to a couple of yes men at Twentieth. To me they said no. Finally I located that agent of mine. He was hard at work in Bel Air. Making with the golf sticks.

Gillis hangs up with a curse, opens the door of the booth, emerges, wiping the sweat from his forehead. He walks towards the exit. He is stopped by the voice of

SKOLSKY
Hello, Gillis.

Gillis looks around. At the fountain sits Skolsky, drinking a cup of coffee.

GILLIS
Hello, Mr. Skolsky.

SKOLSKY
Got anything for the column?

GILLIS
Sure. Just sold an original for a hundred grand. The Life of the Warner Brothers. Starring the Ritz Brothers. Playing opposite the Andrew Sisters.

SKOLSKY
(With a sour smile)
But don't get me wrong -- I love Hollywood.

Gillis walks out.

DISSOLVE TO:

A-14 THE BEL AIR GOLF LINKS

On a sun-dappled green edged with tall sycamores, stands Morino, the agent, a caddy and a nondescript opponent in the background. Gillis has evidently stated his problem already.

Sidney Skolsky's (left) appearance at the drugstore counter was another nod to real-life Hollywood: His column in *Photoplay* magazine had the byline "From a Stool at Schwab's." It is he who was credited with making the drugstore famous, in part by promulgating the myth that Lana Turner was discovered there.

Scene A-13, Schwab's Drugstore

Behind the Scenes

Scene A-14, The Bel Air Golf Links

opposite top: Billy Wilder (behind the counter) chats with William Holden and Sidney Skolsky on the Schwab's Drugstore set.

opposite bottom: Billy talks through the scene with Sidney.

above: The crew sets up the putt that opens Scene A-14.

MORINO
So you need three hundred dollars? Of course, I could give you three hundred dollars. Only I'm not going to.

GILLIS
No?

MORINO
Gillis, get this through your head. I'm not just your agent. It's not the ten per cent. I'm your <u>friend</u>.

He sinks his putt and walks toward the next tee, Gillis following him.

GILLIS
How's that about your being my friend?

MORINO
Don't you know the finest things in the world have been written on an empty stomach? Once a talent like yours gets into that Mocambo-Romanoff rut, you're through.

GILLIS
Forget Romanoff's. It's the car I'm talking about. If I lose my car it's like having my legs cut off.

MORINO
Greatest thing that could happen to you. Now you'll <u>have</u> to sit behind that typewriter. Now you'll <u>have</u> to write.

GILLIS
What do you think I've been doing? I need three hundred dollars.

MORINO
(Icily)
Maybe what you need is another agent.

He bends down to tee up his ball. Gillis turns away.

DISSOLVE TO:

3/19/49

SCENE A-14

A-15 GILLIS IN HIS OPEN CAR

driving down Sunset towards Hollywood. He drives slowly. His mind is working.

GILLIS' VOICE
As I drove back towards town I took inventory of me and my prospects. The whole thing added up to a little less than zero. So I started composing a letter. To W. W. Forbes, Managing Editor, the Dayton Evening Post. Dear Mr. Halitosis: I've just been offered a seven-year contract at five thousand a week. However, I don't think this tinsel town is the place for an upstanding young American, so what about my getting back that thirty-five-dollar-a-week job behind the rewrite desk, you stuffy, mean, penny-pinching, slave-driving... Excuse me just a moment. A couple of friends of mine have just popped up.

Gillis stops his car at a red light by the main entrance to Bel Air. Suddenly his eyes fall on:

A-16 ANOTHER CAR

It is a dark-green Dodge business coupe, also waiting for the light to change, but headed in the opposite direction. In it are the two finance company men. They spot Gillis in his car and exchange looks. From across the intersection Gillis recognizes them and pulls down the leather sunshade to screen his face. As the light changes, Gillis gives his car the gun and shoots away. The men narrowly avoid hitting another car as they make a U-turn into oncoming traffic and start after him.

A-17 to A-21 THE CHASE

Very short, very sharp, told in FLASHES. (Use locations on Sunset between Bel Air and Holmby Hills). The men lose Gillis around a bend, catch sight of him and then -- while they are trapped behind a slow-moving truck, he disappears again.

SCENE A-15

A-22 GILLIS

He is driving as fast as he dares, keeping an eye out for pursuit in his rear-view mirror. Suddenly his right front tire blows out. Gillis clutches desperately at the steering wheel and manages to turn the careening car into

A-23 A DRIVEWAY

It is overgrown with weeds and screened from the street by bushes and trees. Gillis stops his car about thirty feet from the street and looks back.

A-24 THE OTHER CAR

shoots past the driveway, still looking for Gillis.

A-25 GILLIS

He gets out of his car to examine the flat tire. Then he looks around to see where he is.

A-26 THE GARAGE

It is an enormous, five-car affair, neglected and empty except for a large, dust-covered Isotta-Fraschini propped up on blocks.

A-27 GILLIS

He gets back into his car and carefully pilots the limping vehicle into one of the stalls. He closes the garage door and walks up the driveway. In idle curiosity he mounts a stone staircase which leads to the garden, CAMERA IN BACK OF HIM. At the top of the steps he sees the somber pile of

GILLIS' VOICE

I had landed myself in the driveway of some big mansion that looked run-down and deserted. At the end of the drive was a lovely sight indeed: a great big empty garage, just standing there going to waste...If ever there was a place to stash away a limping car with a hot license number...

There was another occupant in that garage: an enormous foreign-built automobile. The kind that burns up ten gallons to a mile. It had a 1932 license. I figured that's when the owners must have moved out.

I also figured it was a cinch I couldn't go back to my apartment, so the thing to do was take a bus for Artie Green's and stay there till I promoted that three hundred dollars.

Gillis: It was a great big white elephant of a place.
The kind of crazy movie people built in the crazy twenties.
A neglected house gets an unhappy look. This one had it in spades.
It was like that old woman from *Great Expectations*.
That Miss Havisham in her rotting wedding dress and torn veil,
taking it out on the world because she'd been given the go-by.
(QUOTE FROM MOVIE, NOT IN SHOOTING SCRIPT)

NORMA DESMOND'S HOUSE.
It is a grandiose, Italianate structure, mottled by the years, gloomy, forsaken, the little formal garden completely gone to seed.

Some people say that when you first see the spot where you're going to die it rings a bell inside you. I didn't hear any bell. It was just big and still, one of those white elephants crazy movie people built in the crazy Twenties.

From somewhere above comes

A WOMAN'S VOICE
You there!

Gillis turns and looks.

A-28 UPSTAIRS LOGGIA

Behind a bamboo blind there is the movement of a dark figure.

WOMAN'S VOICE
Why are you so late? Why have you kept me waiting so long?

A-29 GILLIS

He stands flabbergasted. A new noise attracts his attention -- the creak of a heavy metal-and-glass door being opened. He turns and sees

A-30 THE ENTRANCE DOOR OF THE HOUSE

Max von Mayerling stands there. He is sixty, and all in black, except for immaculate white cotton gloves, shirt, high, stiff collar and a white bow tie. His coat is shiny black alpaca, his trousers ledger-striped. He is semi-paralyzed. The left side of his mouth is pulled down, and he leans on a rubber-ferruled stick.

MAX
In here!

Gillis enters the shot.

GILLIS
I just put my car in the garage. I had a blow-out. I thought --

MAX
Go on in.

There is authority in the gesture of his white-gloved hand as he motions Gillis inside.

GILLIS
Look, maybe I'd better take my car --

MAX
Wipe your feet!

Automatically, Gillis wipes his feet on an enormous shabby cocoanut mat.

MAX
You are not dressed properly.

GILLIS
Dressed for what?

THE WOMAN'S VOICE
Max! Have him come up, Max!

MAX
(Gesturing)
Up the stairs!

GILLIS
Suppose you listen just for a minute --

MAX
Madame is waiting.

GILLIS
For me? Okay.

Gillis enters.

A-31 INT. NORMA DESMOND'S ENTRANCE HALL

It is grandiose and grim. The whole place is one of those abortions of silent-picture days, with bowling alleys in the cellar and a built-in pipe organ, and beams imported from Italy, with California termites at work on them. Portieres are drawn before all the windows, and only thin slits of sunlight find their way in to fight the few electric bulbs which are always burning.

3-19-49

Gillis starts up the curve of the black marble staircase. It has a wrought-iron rail and a worn velvet rope along the wall.

MAX
(From below)
If you need help with the coffin call me.

The oddity of the situation has caught Gillis' imagination. He climbs the stairs with a kind of morbid fascination. At the top he stops, undecided, then turns to the right and is stopped by

WOMAN'S VOICE
This way!

Gillis swings around.

Norma Desmond stands down the corridor next to a doorway from which emerges a flickering light. She is a little woman. There is a curious style, a great sense of high voltage about her. She is dressed in black house pyjamas and black high-heeled pumps. Around her throat there is a leopard-patterned scarf, and wound around her head a turban of the same material. Her skin is very pale, and she is wearing dark glasses.

NORMA
In here. I put him on my massage table in front of the fire. He always liked fires and poking at them with a stick.

Gillis enters the SHOT and she leads him into

A-32 NORMA DESMOND'S BEDROOM

It is a huge, gloomy room hung in white brocade which has become dirty over the years and even slightly torn in a few places. There's a great, unmade gilded bed in the shape of a swan, from which the gold had begun to peel. There is a disorder of clothes and negligees and faded photographs of old-time stars about.

In an imitation baroque fireplace some logs are burning. On the massage table before it lies a small form shrouded under a Spanish shawl. At each end on a baroque pedestal stands a three-branched candelabrum, the candles lighted.

NORMA
I've made up my mind we'll bury him in the garden. Any city laws against that?

SCENE A-32

SCENE A-32

11454-6

SCENE A-32

Gillis: I know your face.
You're Norma Desmond.
You used to be in pictures.
You used to be big.

GILLIS
I wouldn't know.

NORMA
I don't care anyway. I want the coffin to be white. And I want it specially lined with satin. White, or deep pink.

She picks up the shawl to make up her mind about the color. From under the shawl flops down a dead arm. Gillis stares and recoils a little. It is like a child's arm, only black and hairy.

NORMA
Maybe red, bright flaming red. Gay. Let's make it gay.

Gillis edges closer and glances down. Under the shawl he sees the sad, bearded face of a dead chimpanzee. Norma drops back the shawl.

NORMA
How much will it be? I warn you - don't give me a fancy price just because I'm rich.

GILLIS
Lady, you've got the wrong man.

For the first time, Norma really looks at him through her dark glasses.

GILLIS
I had some trouble with my car. Flat tire. I pulled into your garage till I could get a spare. I thought this was an empty house.

NORMA
It is not. Get out.

GILLIS
I'm sorry, and I'm sorry you lost your friend, and I don't think red is the right color.

NORMA
Get out.

GILLIS
Sure. Wait a minute -- haven't I seen you --?

NORMA
Or shall I call my servant?

GILLIS
I know your face. You're Norma Desmond. You used to be in pictures. You used to be big.

NORMA
I *am* big. It's the pictures that got small.

GILLIS
I knew there was something wrong with them.

NORMA
They're dead. They're finished. There was a time when this business had the eyes of the whole wide world. But that wasn't good enough. Oh, no! They wanted the ears of the world, too. So they opened their big mouths, and out came talk, talk, talk ...

GILLIS
That's where the popcorn business comes in. You buy yourself a bag and plug up your ears.

NORMA
Look at them in the front offices -- the master minds! They took the idols and smashed them. The Fairbankses and the Chaplins and the Gilberts and the Valentinos. And who have they got now? Some nobodies -- a lot of pale little frogs croaking pish-posh!

GILLIS
Don't get sore at me. I'm not an executive. I'm just a writer.

NORMA
You are! Writing words, words! You've made a rope of words and strangled this business! But there is a microphone right there to catch the last gurgles, and Technicolor to photograph the red, swollen tongue!

3-19-49

GILLIS
Ssh! You'll wake up that monkey.

NORMA
Get out!

Gillis starts down the stairs.

GILLIS
Next time I'll bring my autograph album along, or maybe a hunk of cement and ask for your footprints.

He is halfway down the staircase when he is stopped by

NORMA
Just a minute, you!

GILLIS
Yeah?

NORMA
You're a writer, you said.

GILLIS
Why?

Norma starts down the stairs.

NORMA
Are you or aren't you?

GILLIS
I think that's what it says on my driver's license.

NORMA
And you have written pictures, haven't you?

GILLIS
Sure have. The last one I wrote was about cattle rustlers. Before they were through with it, the whole thing played on a torpedo boat.

Norma has reached him at the bottom of the staircase.

NORMA
I want to ask you something. Come in here.

She leads him into

3-19-49

A-33 THE HUGE LIVING ROOM

It is dark and damp and filled with black oak and red velvet furniture which looks like crappy props from the Mark of Zorro set. Along the main wall, a gigantic fireplace has been freezing for years. On the gold piano is a galaxy of photographs of Norma Desmond in her various roles. On one wall is a painting -- a California Gold Rush scene, Carthay Circle school. (We will learn later that it hides a motion picture screen.)

One corner is filled with a large pipe organ, and as Norma and Gillis enter, there is a grizzly moaning sound. Gillis looks around.

NORMA
The wind gets in that blasted pipe organ. I ought to have it taken out.

GILLIS
Or teach it a better tune.

Norma has led him to the card tables which stand side by side near a window. They are piled high with papers scrawled in a large, uncertain hand.

NORMA
How long is a movie script these days? I mean, how many pages?

GILLIS
Depends on what it is -- a Donald Duck or Joan of Arc.

NORMA
This is to be a very important picture. I have written it myself. Took me years.

GILLIS
(Looking at the piles of script)
Looks like enough for six important pictures.

NORMA
It's the story of Salome. I think I'll have DeMille direct it.

GILLIS
Uh-huh.

SCENE A-33

Gillis: I didn't know you were planning a comeback.
Norma: I hate that word. It is a return.
A return to the millions of people who have never
forgiven me for deserting the screen.

NORMA
We've made a lot of pictures
together.

GILLIS
And you'll play Salome?

NORMA
Who else?

GILLIS
Only asking. I didn't know
you were planning a comeback.

NORMA
I hate that word. It is a return.
A return to the millions of people
who have never forgiven me for
deserting the screen.

GILLIS
Fair enough.

NORMA
Salome -- what a woman! What a
part! The Princess in love with
a Holy Man. She dances the Dance
of the Seven Veils. He rejects
her, so she demands his head on a
golden tray, kissing his cold, dead
lips.

GILLIS
They'll love it in Pomona.

NORMA
(Taking it straight)
They will love it every place.
(She reaches for a
batch of pages from
the heap)
Read it. Read the scene just
before she has him killed!

GILLIS
Right now? Never let another
writer read your stuff. He
may steal it.

NORMA
I am not afraid. Read it!

NORMA (Cont'd)
(Calling)
Max! Max!
(To Gillis)
Sit down. Is there enough light?

GILLIS
I've got twenty-twenty vision.

Max has entered.

NORMA
Bring something to drink.

MAX
Yes, Madame.

He leaves. Norma turns to Gillis again.

NORMA
I said sit down.

There is compulsion in her voice.

Gillis looks at her and starts slowly reading.	GILLIS' VOICE She had a voice like a ring-master's whip. Somehow I found myself sitting there reading that mad scrawl of hers. Some letters big and arrogant, others as small as fly-specks. I wondered what a handwriting expert would
Max comes in, wheeling a wicker tea wagon on which are two bottles of champagne and two red Venetian glasses, a box of zwieback and a jar of caviar. Norma sits on her feet, deep in a chair, a gold ring on her forefinger with a clip which holds a cigarette. She gets up and forces on Gillis another batch of script, goes back to her chair.	make of it. Max wheeled in some champagne and some caviar. Later, I found out that Max was the only other person in that grim Sunset castle of hers, and I found out a few other things about him. As for her, she sat there curled up like a watch spring. I could sense her eyes on me behind those dark glasses. She kept smoking some Turkish brand of cigarettes. There was a contraption she used to hold them, so her yellow fingers wouldn't get more yellow ...

11454-47

Behind the Scenes

Scene A-33, The Huge Living Room

William Holden (Gillis) talks over the scene with Erich von Stroheim (Max) between takes.

A-34 SHOT OF THE CEILING

PAN DOWN to the moaning organ. PAN OVER TO THE ENTRANCE DOOR. Max opens it, and a solemn-faced man in undertaker's clothes brings in a small white coffin. (Thru these shots the room has been growing duskier).

GILLIS' VOICE
It sure was a cozy set-up--Max and she and that dead monkey upstairs, and the wind wheezing through that organ once in a while. Later on, just for comedy relief, the real guy arrived, with a baby coffin. It was all done with great dignity. He must have been a very important chimp. The great grandson of King Kong, maybe ...

DISSOLVE TO:

A-35 GILLIS

reading. The lamp beside him is now really paying its way in the dark room. A lot of the manuscript pages are piled on the floor around his feet. A half-empty champagne glass stands on the arm of his chair.

It got to be eleven o'clock. I was feeling a little sick at my stomach. It wasn't just that sweet champagne. It was wading through that guck of hers, that mad hodge-podge of melodramatic plots. However, by then I'd started concocting a little plot of my own ...

THE CAMERA SLOWLY DRAWS BACK to include Norma Desmond sitting in the dusk, just as she was before. Gillis puts down a batch of script. There is a little pause.

NORMA
(Impatiently)
Well?

GILLIS
This is fascinating.

NORMA
Of course it is.

GILLIS
Maybe it's a little long and maybe there are some repetitions... but you're not a professional writer.

SCENE A-35

Gillis: What it needs is a little more dialogue.
Norma: What for? I can say anything I want with my eyes.

NORMA
I wrote that with my heart.

GILLIS
Sure you did. That's what makes it great. What it needs is a little more dialogue.

NORMA
What for? I can say anything I want with my eyes.

GILLIS
It certainly could use a pair of shears and a blue pencil.

NORMA
I will not have it butchered.

GILLIS
Of course not. But it ought to be organized. Just an editing job. You can find somebody ---

NORMA
Who?
(There is a pregnant pause)
When were you born -- I mean what sign of the zodiac?

GILLIS
I don't know.

NORMA
What month?

GILLIS
December twenty-first.

NORMA
Sagittarius. I like Sagittarians.

GILLIS
Thank you.

NORMA
I want you to do this work.

GILLIS
Me? I'm busy. Just finished one script. I'm due on another assignment.

NORMA
I don't care.

GILLIS
You know, I'm pretty expensive.
I get five hundred a week.

NORMA
I wouldn't worry about money.
I'll make it worth your while.

GILLIS
Maybe I'd better finish reading it.

NORMA
You'll read it tonight.

GILLIS
It's getting kind of late --

NORMA
(Out of nowhere)
Are you married, Mr. -- ?

GILLIS
The name is Gillis. I'm single.

NORMA
Where do you live?

GILLIS
In Hollywood. The Alto Nido
Apartments.

NORMA
There's something wrong with your
car, you said.

GILLIS
There sure is.

NORMA
(Calling)
Max!
(To Gillis)
You're staying here.

GILLIS
I am?

Norma takes off her glasses.

NORMA
Yes, you are. There's a room
over the garage. Max!

THE CAMERA MOVES TOWARD NORMA'S FACE, right up to her eyes.

GILLIS' VOICE
She sure could say a lot of things with those pale eyes of hers. They'd been her trade mark. They'd made her the Number One Vamp of another era. I remember a rather florid description in an old fan magazine which said: "Her eyes are like two moonlit waterholes, where strange animals come to drink."

DISSOLVE TO:

A-36 SMALL STAIRCASE, LEADING TO ROOM OVER GARAGE

Max, an electric light bulb in his hand, is leading Gillis up. Gillis carries a batch of the manuscript.

GILLIS' VOICE
I took the rest of the script and Max led me to the room over the garage. I thought I'd wangled myself a pretty good deal. I'd do a little work, my car would be safe down below, until I got some money out of her...

Max pushes open a door at the top of the stairs.

MAX
(Opening the door)
I made your bed this afternoon.

GILLIS
Thanks.
(On second thought)
How did you know I was going to stay, this afternoon?

Max doesn't answer. He walks across to the bed, screws a bulb in the open socket above it. The light goes on, revealing:

A-37 A GABLED BEDROOM

There are dirty windows on two sides, and dingy wallpaper on the cracked plaster walls. For furniture there is a neatly made bed, a table and a few chairs which might have been discarded from the main house.

MAX
This room has not been used for a long time.

GILLIS
It will never make House Beautiful. I guess it's O.K. for one night.

Max gives him an enigmatic look.

MAX
(Pointing)
There is the bathroom. I put in soap and a toothbrush.

GILLIS
Thanks.
(He starts taking off his coat)
Say, she's quite a character, that Norma Desmond.

MAX

She was the greatest. You wouldn't know. You are too young. In one week she got seventeen thousand fan letters. Men would bribe her manicurist to get clippings from her fingernails. There was a Maharajah who came all the way from Hyderabad to get one of her stockings. Later, he strangled himself with it.

GILLIS

I sure turned into an interesting driveway.

MAX

You did, sir.

He goes out. Gillis looks after him, hangs his coat over a chair, walks over to the window, pulls down the rickety Venetian blind. As he does so, he looks down at:

GILLIS' VOICE

I figured he was a little crazy. Maybe he'd had a stroke -- part of his brain wasn't hitting on all cylinders. Come to think of it, the whole place was like that -- half paralyzed, crumbling apart in slow motion.

A-38 THE TENNIS COURT OF THE DESMOND HOUSE (MOONLIGHT)

The cement surface is cracked in many places, and weeds are growing high.

GILLIS' VOICE

There was a tennis court, or rather the ghost of a tennis court, with faded markings and a sagging net.

A-39 GILLIS - IN THE WINDOW

He looks away from the court to;

A-40 THE DESMOND SWIMMING POOL

There is no water in it, and hunks of mosaic which lines its enormous basin are broken away.

And of course she had a pool. Who didn't then? Mabel Normand and John Gilbert must have swum in it ten thousand midnights ago, and Vilma Banky and Rod LaRoque. It was empty now, except for some rubbish and something stirring down there ...

A-41 GILLIS - IN THE WINDOW

He stares down, his stomach slowly turning.

A-42 THE SWIMMING POOL

At the bottom of the basin a great rat is eating a decaying orange. From the inlet pipe crawl two other rats, who join battle with the first rat over the orange.

A-43 GILLIS - IN THE WINDOW

He starts away, but something attracts his attention. He turns back and looks down again.

GILLIS' VOICE
I thought I caught the flicker of a light. There was something else going on below -- the last rites for that hairy old chimp. She was always playing some sort of part. This time she was Lady Macbeth on a tragic Scottish moor, or a bereaved empress queen mourning her dead prince imperial...

A-44 THE LAWN BELOW

Norma Desmond and Max are carrying the white coffin towards a small grave which has been dug in the dead turf. Norma carries one of the candelabra, all of its candles flickering in the wind. They reach the grave and lower the coffin into it. Then, Norma lighting his task with the candelabrum, Max takes a spade from the loose earth and starts filling in the grave.

A-45 GILLIS - IN THE WINDOW

He watches the scene below, then turns into the room, goes to the door to lock it. There is no key, and only a hole where the lock has been gouged out. Gillis moves a heavy overstuffed chair in front of the door, then walks towards the bed, throws himself on it, picking up some of the manuscript pages to read.

GILLIS' VOICE
It was all very queer, but queerer things were yet to come...!

DISSOLVE:

END OF SEQUENCE "A"

SCENE A-44

BB 2nd Change SUNSET BOULEVARD 7-19-49 33.

SEQUENCE "B"

DISSOLVE IN ON:

B-1 LONG SHOT THE DESMOND HOUSE - (MORNING)

The day is overcast. The house is shrouded in low fog.

SOUND: (Distant organ music - improvisations on an odd, mournful theme - not too loud, continuing throughout the scene.)

B-2 THE TENNIS COURT, blurred over with fog.

B-3 THE EMPTY SWIMMING POOL its dark outline even more melancholy under the misty blanket.

B-4 THE ROOM OVER THE GARAGE

Muted daylight seeps through the blinds. Gillis lies on the bed, under a shabby quilt. The manuscript is beside him, some of the pages scattered on the floor. He is just opening his eyes. It takes him a moment to adjust himself to the strange surroundings. His eyes, wandering about the room, suddenly stop, startled. He lifts himself on one elbow and stares at -

GILLIS' V. VOICE

There was organ music seeping into my dreams. It was like waking up in a belfry with mass going on below and Johann Sebastian Bach begging God to forgive us all our sins.

B-5 THE DOOR

The heavy chair he had set against it the night before has been pushed back. The door is wide ajar.

Oh sure, I was in that empty room over her garage. Only it wasn't empty anymore. I'd had a visitor.

B-6 GILLIS

He jumps out of bed. He wears, shirt, trousers and socks. He goes to the door and looks outside, then turns back to the room. Suddenly he realizes that all his

Somebody had brought in all my belongings...my books, my typewriter, my clothes....

Scene B-7, The Big Room

Swanson and von Stroheim get their final touch-ups before filming Scene B-7.

possessions have been brought in. In the closet hang his shirts. His books and typewriter are neatly arranged on the table. His phonograph-radio combination is all installed. Gillis looks around startled, then sits down and starts putting on his moccasins hastily.

GILLIS' VOICE
What was going on?

DISSOLVE TO:

B-7 A PAIR OF HANDS IN WHITE GLOVES, PLAYING THE ORGAN

PULL BACK: They belong to Max von Mayerling. He is sitting erect, his bull neck taut as a wrestler's as he fights out somber chord after somber chord. He sits in a shaft of gray light coming from an open French window.

Through the far archway, Gillis storms into the big room.

GILLIS
Hey, you -- Max -- whatever -your-name-is -- what are my things doing here?

No answer.

GILLIS
I'm talking to you. My clothes and things are up in the room.

MAX
Naturally. I brought them myself.

GILLIS
(Furiously)
Is that so!

MAX
Why are you so upset? Is there anything missing?

GILLIS
Who said you could? Who asked you to?

Norma Desmond's shadow moves into the shaft of light.

SCENE B-7

Behind the Scenes

Scene B-7, The Big Room

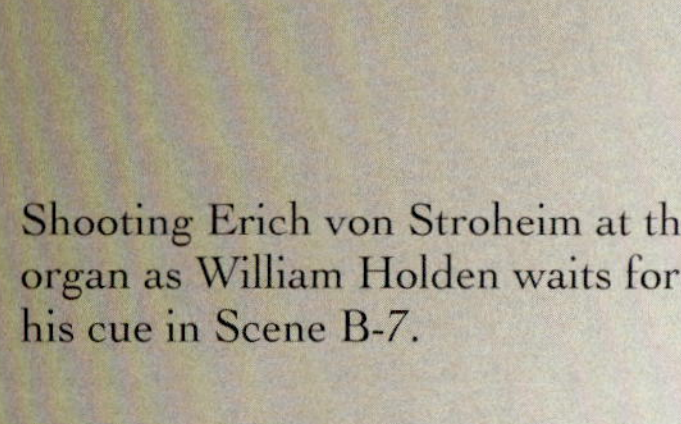

Shooting Erich von Stroheim at the organ as William Holden waits for his cue in Scene B-7.

90
11454-2/M38

SCENE B-7

NORMA'S VOICE
I did.

Gillis looks around.

On the couch by the fireplace reclines Norma Desmond, dressed in a negligee. She rises.

NORMA
I don't know why you should be so upset. Stop that playing, Max.
(To Gillis again)
It seemed like a good idea -- if we are to work together.

GILLIS
Look, I'm supposed to fix up your script. There's nothing in the deal about my staying here.

NORMA
You'll like it here.

GILLIS
Thanks for the invitation, but I have my own apartment.

NORMA
You can't work in an apartment where you owe three months' rent.

GILLIS
I'll take care of that.

NORMA
It's all taken care of. It's all paid for.

GILLIS
I'm used to paying my own bills.

NORMA
You proud boy, why didn't you tell me you were having difficulties.

GILLIS
Okay. We'll deduct it from my salary.

NORMA
Now, now, don't let's be small about such matters. We won't keep books.
(To Max)
Go on, unpack Mr. Gillis' things.

GILLIS
Unpack nothing. I didn't say I was staying.

NORMA
(Her glasses off again)
Suppose you make up your mind. Do you want this job or don't you?

DISSOLVE TO:

B-8 BIG ROOM, NORMA DESMOND'S HOUSE - (DAY)

Gillis sits at an improvised table, his typewriter in front of him, working hard at the manuscript. Pencils, shears and a paste-pot at hand.

Facing him at some distance sits Norma, dressed in another version of her favorite lounging pajamas, the cigarette contraption on her finger. She is autographing large photographs of herself and putting them in envelopes.

GILLIS' VOICE
Yes, I wanted the job. I wanted the dough, and I wanted to get out of there as quickly as I could. I thought if I really got going I could toss it off in a couple of weeks. But it wasn't so simple, getting some coherence into those wild hallucinations of hers. And what made it even worse was that she was around all the time, hovering over me, afraid I'd do injury to that precious brain-child of hers.

Gillis takes two or three pages from Norma's handwritten script, crosses them out and puts them to one side.

Norma rises, crosses towards Gillis, looks over his shoulder.

NORMA
What's that?

GILLIS
Just a scene I cut out.

SCENE B-8

Gillis: I thought if I really got going I could
toss it off in a couple of weeks. But it wasn't so simple,
getting some coherence into those wild hallucinations of hers.

NORMA
What scene?

GILLIS
The one where you go to the slave market. You can cut right to the scene where John the Baptist --

NORMA
Cut away from me?

GILLIS
Honestly, it's a little old hat. They don't want that any more.

NORMA
They don't? Then why do they still write me fan letters every day. Why do they beg me for my photographs? Because they want to see me, me, me! Norma Desmond.

GILLIS
(Resigned)
Okay.

He pulls the page from his typewriter. As he does so he glances over towards Norma.

On the table in front of her are the photographs which she is signing. On the long table in the living room is a gallery of photographs in various frames -- all Norma Desmond. On the piano more photographs. Above the piano an oil portrait of her. On the highboy beside him still more photographs.

GILLIS' VOICE
Norma Desmond! Sometimes I felt I couldn't breathe in that room, it was so thick with Norma Desmonds. Staring at me, crowding me, stampeding me - Norma Desmonds, more Norma Desmonds, and still more Norma Desmonds.

DISSOLVE TO:

SCENE B-9

1145 4-4

11454-55

Scene B-11, The Projection Booth

Billy Wilder peering out of the projection room port in Norma's living room. It is from here that the light will shine to simulate a film being projected in the scene.

B-9 THE BIG ROOM (NIGHT)

Shooting towards the big Gold Rush painting. Max, white gloves and all, steps into the shot, shoves the painting up towards the ceiling, revealing a motion picture screen. Max exits.

GILLIS' VOICE

It wasn't all work, of course. About two or three times a week Max would haul up that enormous oil painting that had been presented to her by some Nevada Chamber of Commerce, and we'd see a movie -- right in her living room.

SCENE B-12

B-10 NORMA AND GILLIS

They sit on a couch, facing the screen. On a table in front of them are champagne, cigarettes and coffee. Above their heads are the typical openings for a projector. The lights go off. From the opening above their heads shoots the wide beam of light.

GILLIS' VOICE
It was all very formal-- a demi-tasse, an after-dinner drink. Loge seats. So much nicer than going out, she used to say.

B-11 MAX, IN THE PROJECTION BOOTH BEHIND THE ROOM

The light of the machine flickering over his face, which is frozen, a somber enigma.

They were silent movies, and Max would run the machine, which was just as well -- it kept him from giving us an accompaniment on that rusty organ.

B-12 NORMA AND GILLIS

watching the screen. Gillis looks down and sees that Norma's hand is clasping his arm tight. He doesn't like it much but he can't do anything about it. However, when she for a second lets go his arm to pick up a glass of champagne, he gently withdraws his arm, leans away from her and crosses his arms to discourage any resumption of her approach. Norma puts the glass down, doesn't find his arm, but is not aware of any significance in his maneuver. They both watch the screen.

She'd sit very close to me and she'd smell of tuberoses, which is not my favorite perfume, not by a long shot. She was always holding me by the arm or by the hand, but I always thought it was just like caressing a dog. Then again maybe it was because she was so excited about that old worn-out celluloid up there on the screen. I guess I don't have to tell you who the star was. They were always her pictures. That's all she ever wanted to see.

B-13 THE OTHER END OF THE BIG ROOM, WITH THE SCREEN

On it flickers a famous scene from one of Norma's old silent pictures. It is not to be a funny scene. It is old-fashioned, but shows her incredible beauty and the screen presence which made her the great star of her day.

SCENE B-14

Norma: Those idiot producers! Those imbeciles! Haven't they got any eyes? Have they forgotten what a star looks like? I'll show them. I'll be up there again. So help me!

11454-65

B-14 NORMA AND GILLIS ON THE COUCH

NORMA
Still wonderful, isn't it? And no dialogue. We didn't need dialogue. We had faces. There just aren't any faces like that any more. Well, maybe one -- Garbo.

In a sudden flareup she jumps to her feet and stands in the flickering beam of light.

NORMA
Those idiot producers! Those imbeciles! Haven't they got any eyes? Have they forgotten what a star looks like? I'll show them. I'll be up there again. So help me!

DISSOLVE TO:

B-15 THE BIG ROOM - (NIGHT)

It is apparently empty. The elaborate lamps make pools of light.

THE CAMERA PULLS BACK AND PANS to reveal a card table around which sit Norma and three friends - three actors of her period. They sit erect and play with grim seriousness.

Beside Norma sits Gillis, kibitzing on a game which bores him extremely. An ashtray on the card table is full and Norma holds it out for Gillis to take away. He crosses the room to the fireplace, but his eyes fall on the entrance door and he stops.

GILLIS' VOICE
Except for those outbursts of hers, it was the quietest house imaginable. The telephone never rang. The door bell never rang. No one ever came. . . No, that's not quite true. Every second Tuesday there'd be a little bridge game in the house, at a twentieth-of-a-cent a point. I'd get half her winnings. Once they ran up to a dollar and seventy cents, which was about the only cash money I ever got. The others around the table would be actor friends, dim figures you may still remember from the silent days. I used to think of them as her wax works.

B-16 THE ENTRANCE HALL - (FROM GILLIS' POINT OF VIEW)

Max stands in the open door. Outside are the two men who came to the apartment for Gillis' car.

SCENE B-15
clockwise from top: The "waxworks." Buster Keaton, Anna Q. Nilsson, H. B. Warner.

Scene B-15, The Big Room
(Night)

above: Wilder talks through the unscripted scene with Swanson, Buster Keaton, and H. B. Warner. A stand-in sits in Anna Q. Nilsson's place at the table.
opposite: Shooting the bridge scene.

1154-2175

B-17 GILLIS

He steps back so that he cannot be seen from the door. A second later Max appears, looking for him.

MAX
(Quietly)
Some men are here. They asked for you.

GILLIS
I'm not here.

MAX
That's what I told them.

GILLIS
Good.

MAX
They found your car in the garage. They are going to tow it away.

Gillis doesn't know what to do. From offstage comes:

NORMA'S VOICE
The ashtray, Joe dear! Can we have the ashtray?

Gillis dumps the cigarette butts into the cold fireplace, crosses to the bridge table, puts the ashtray down, leans over and speaks into Norma's ear.

GILLIS
I want to talk to you for a minute.

NORMA
Not now, my dear. I'm playing three no trump.

GILLIS
They've come for my car.

NORMA
Please. Now I've forgotten how many spades are out.

GILLIS
I need some money right now.

NORMA
Can't you wait till I'm dummy?

3-22-49

GILLIS
No.

SCENE B-17

NORMA
(Angry by now)
Please!

Gillis stands frustrated, hideously embarrassed by the stares of the waxworks. He turns away and hurries to the door.

B-18 ENTRANCE DOOR TO THE HOUSE

It is half open. Gillis comes into the shot and, taking cover, looks out.

B-19 COURTYARD (FROM GILLIS' ANGLE)

The men from the finance company are cranking up the car. Max stands watching silently. When they finish the cranking job, the men climb into the front seat of the truck.

B-20 GILLIS - IN THE DOOR

Over the shot the SOUND of the truck being started and the cars moving away. Gillis moves out into the courtyard and stands staring after the car. From the house comes Norma.

NORMA
Now what is it? Where's the fire?

GILLIS
I've lost my car.

NORMA
Oh...and I thought it was a matter of life and death.

GILLIS
It is to me. That's why I came to this house. That's why I took this job -- ghost writing!

NORMA
Now you're being silly. We don't need two cars. We have a car. And not one of those cheap new things made of chromium and spit. An Isotta-Fraschini. Have you ever heard of Isotta-Fraschinis? All hand-made. Cost me twenty-eight thousand dollars.

SCENE B-20

Gillis: I've lost my car.
Norma: Oh . . . and I thought it was
a matter of life and death.

SCENE B-22

THE CAMERA HAS PANNED over to the garage and FOCUSES on the dirty Isotta-Fraschini on its blocks.

DISSOLVE TO:

B-21 NORMA'S ISOTTA-FRASCHINI DRIVING IN THE HILLS ABOVE SUNSET (DAY)

Max is at the wheel, dressed as usual except for a chauffeur's cap.

GILLIS' VOICE
So Max got that old bus down off its blocks and polished it up. She'd take me for rides in the hills above Sunset.

The whole thing was upholstered in leopard skin, and had one of those car phones, all gold-plated.

B-22 INSIDE THE CAR

Gillis sits beside Norma, who is wearing a smart tailleur and her eternal sun glasses. Gillis wears his sport jacket-flannel trousers-moccasin combination.

He sits uncomfortably. Norma is studying him.

NORMA
That's a dreadful shirt you're wearing.

GILLIS
What's wrong with it?

NORMA
Nothing, if you work in a filling station. And I'm getting rather bored with that sport jacket, and those same baggy pants.
(She picks up the car phone)
Max, what's a good men's shop in town? The very best.... Well, go there!

GILLIS
I don't need any clothes, and I certainly don't want you buying them for --

NORMA
Why begrudge me a little fun?
I just want you to look nice,
my stray little boy.

By this time Max has made a U-turn.

QUICK DISSOLVE TO:

B-23 INT. MEN'S DEPARTMENT - AN ELEGANT WILSHIRE STORE

Gillis stands in front of a full-length triple mirror, surrounded by a couple of salesmen and the tailor, who is busily working out alterations.

Gillis wears a double-breasted gray flannel coat with chalk stripes. His trousers belong to another suit of glen plaid. Norma is running the show.

NORMA
There's nothing like gray
flannel with a chalk stripe.
(She points at
the trousers)
This one single-breasted, of course.
(To another salesman)
Now we need a topcoat. Let's see
what you have in camel's hair.

The salesman leaves.

NORMA
How about some evening clothes?

GILLIS
I don't need a tuxedo.

NORMA
Of course you do. A tuxedo and
tails.

GILLIS
Tails. That's ridiculous.

NORMA
You'll need them for parties.
You'll need them for New Year's
Eve.
(To a salesman)
Where are your evening clothes?

SALESMAN
This way, Madame.

He leads her off. The other salesman arrives with a selection of topcoats.

SALESMAN
Here are some camel hairs, but I'd like you just to feel this one. It's Vicuna. Of course, it's a little more expensive.

GILLIS
A camel's hair will do.

SALESMAN
(With an insulting inflection)
As long as the lady is paying for it, why not take the Vicuna?

DISSOLVE:

END OF SEQUENCE "B"

3-22-49

SCENE B-23

Salesman: As long as the lady is paying for it, why not take the Vicuna?

11454-3

MB 1st Change SUNSET BOULEVARD 7-19-49 45.

SEQUENCE "C"

DISSOLVE IN:

C-1 LONG SHOT DESMOND HOUSE

A day in December. Rain.

QUICK DISSOLVE TO:

C-2 INT. ROOM OVER GARAGE

Water is drizzling from two or three spots in the ceiling into pans and bowls set to catch it, one bowl right on the bed. The room is almost emptied of Gillis' belongings by now. Max is carrying out a handful of new suits on hangers. He has a dressing gown over his shoulder. Gillis holds a stack of shirts, his typewriter, and some manuscript. He surveys the room for the last time, to see whether he's forgotten anything. He has. He puts down the typewriter and picks up from under the bed a pair of very smart red leather bedroom slippers. He tucks them under his arm, picks up the typewriter and leaves.

GILLIS' VOICE
The last week in December the rains came -- a great big package of rain. Over-sized, like everything else in California.

It came right through the old roof of my room above the garage. She had Max move me to the main house. I didn't much like the idea -- the only time I could have to myself was in that room -- but it was better than sleeping in a raincoat and galoshes.

QUICK DISSOLVE TO:

C-3 A BEDROOM IN THE MAIN HOUSE

It is obviously a man's room -- heavy Spanish furniture. One wall is nothing but a closet with shelves and drawers for shirts and shoes. Max is hanging up the suits. Gillis throws the shirts on a big chair, tosses the slippers at the foot of the bed, places the typewriter and manuscript on a desk at the window.

Anyway, it was dry in the big house, even though it smelled close and musty. Generations of moths had grown fat off the carpet.

SCENE C-2

GILLIS
Whose room was this?

MAX
It was the room of the husband. Or of the <u>husbands</u>, I should say. Madame has been married three times.

Slightly embarrassed, Gillis picks up his toilet kit with razor, toothbrushes, soap, etc., and starts towards the bathroom, pausing en route at a rain-splattered window.

GILLIS
I guess this is the one you can see Catalina from. Only this isn't the day.

He proceeds towards the half-opened door leading to the bathroom. Something strikes his attention and he stops. As in the door to the room above the garage, this lock, too, has been gouged out.

GILLIS
Hey, what's this with the door? There isn't any lock.

MAX
There are no locks anywhere in this house.

He points to the entrance door of the room, and to another door.

GILLIS
How come?

MAX
The doctor suggested it.

GILLIS
What doctor?

MAX
Madame's doctor. She has moments of melancholy. There have been some suicide attempts.

GILLIS
Uh-huh?

SCENE C-3

Max: We have to be very careful.
No sleeping pills, no razor blades.
We shut off the gas in her bedroom.
Joe: Why? Her career? She got enough out of it.
She's not forgotten. She still gets those fan letters.
Max: I wouldn't look too closely at the postmarks.

MAX
We have to be very careful. No sleeping pills, no razor blades. We shut off the gas in her bedroom.

GILLIS
Why? Her career? She got enough out of it. She's not forgotten. She still gets those fan letters.

MAX
I wouldn't look too closely at the postmarks.

GILLIS
You send them. Is that it, Max?

MAX
I'd better press your evening clothes, sir. You have not forgotten Madame's New Year's party.

GILLIS
No, I haven't. I suppose all the waxworks are coming?

MAX
I don't know, sir. Madame made the arrangements.

Max leaves. Gillis comes out of the bathroom, picks up his shirts, goes over to a closet, opens it. As he does so one of the doors without a lock swings slightly open. Gillis looks through the half-open door and sees.

C-4 NORMA DESMOND'S ROOM

It is empty. The rainy day does nothing to help its gloom.

GILLIS' VOICE
There it was again -- that room of hers, all satin and ruffles, and that bed like a gilded rowboat. The perfect setting for a silent movie queen. Poor devil, still waving proudly to a parade which had long since passed her by.

He pushes the door shut and walks back into the room.

DISSOLVE TO:

C-5 STAIRCASE OF DESMOND HOUSE (NIGHT)

Gillis is coming down the stairs in his tailcoat, adjusting the handkerchief in his pocket. He obviously feels a little uneasy in this outfit. From below comes a tango of the Twenties, played by a small orchestra. Gillis stops in the archway leading to the big room and looks around.

GILLIS' VOICE
So she was giving a New Year's Eve party, for me and those silent friends of hers...Well, she'd certainly gone to town....I hadn't expected anything like this....

C-6 THE BIG ROOM has been decorated for the occasion with laurel garlands. Dozens of candles in all the sconces and candelabra are ablaze. Their flickering flames are reflected in the waxed surface of the tile floor. There is a buffet, with buckets of champagne and caviar on ice. In one corner, on a little platform banked with palms, a four-piece orchestra is playing.

At the buffet are Max and Norma. She is drinking a glass of champagne. She is wearing a diamonte evening dress, very high style, with long black gloves and a headdress of paradise feathers. Her eyes fall on Gillis. She puts down the glass of champagne, picks up a gardenia boutonniere and moves toward him.

NORMA
Joe, you look absolutely divine. Turn around!

GILLIS
(Embarrassed)
Please.

NORMA
Come on!

Gillis makes a slow 360-degree turn.

NORMA
Perfect. Wonderful shoulders. And I love that line.

SCENE C-6

Norma: Perfect. Wonderful shoulders.
And I love that line.
Joe: All padding. Don't let it fool you.

She indicates the V from his shoulders to his hips.

GILLIS
All padding. Don't let it fool you.

NORMA
Come here!

She puts the gardenia on his lapel.

GILLIS
You know, to me dressing up was always just putting on my dark blue suit.

NORMA
I don't like those studs they've sent. I want you to have pearls. Nice big pearls.

GILLIS
Now, I'm not going to wear ear-rings, I can tell you that.

NORMA
Cute. Let's have some drinks.

She leads him over to the buffet.

GILLIS
Shouldn't we wait for the others?

NORMA
(Pointing at the floor)
Careful, it's slippery. I had it waxed.

They reach the buffet. Max is ready with two glasses of champagne. Norma hands Gillis a glass.

NORMA
Here's to us.

They drink.

NORMA
You know, this floor used to be wood but I had it changed. Valentino said there is nothing like tiles for a tango.

She opens her arms.

3-22-49

GILLIS
Not on the same floor with Valentino!

NORMA
Just follow me.

They start to tango. After a moment --

NORMA
Don't bend back like that.

GILLIS
It's those feathers. They tickle.

Norma pulls the paradise feathers from her hair and tosses them away.

C-7 THE ORCHESTRA

As they play the tango, the musicians eye the dancing couple, take in the situation, exchange glances and turn away with professional discretion.

C-8 NORMA AND GILLIS, TANGOING

Gillis glances at his wrist watch.

GILLIS
It's a quarter past ten. What time are they supposed to get here?

NORMA
Who?

GILLIS
The other guests?

NORMA
There are no other guests. We don't want to share this night with other people. This is for you and me.

GILLIS
I understand some rich guy bought up all the tickets for a performance at the Metropolitan and sat there listening to La Traviata, all by himself. He was afraid of catching cold.

3-22-49

SCENE C-6

11454-4

SCENE C-6

NORMA
Hold me tighter.

GILLIS
Come midnight, how about blindfolding the orchestra and smashing champagne glasses on Max's head?

NORMA
You think this is all very funny.

GILLIS
A little.

NORMA
Is it funny that I'm in love with you?

GILLIS
What's that?

NORMA
I'm in love with you. Don't you know that? I've been in love with you all along.

They dance on. Gillis is acutely embarrassed. THE CAMERA SLOWLY PULLS BACK, PANS past the faces of the musicians, who play on with a rather overemphasized lack of interest. Finally it winds up on Max, behind the buffet. He stands watching Gillis, a faint trace of pity in his eyes.

DISSOLVE TO:

C-9	NORMA'S FINGER, WITH THE CIGARETTE GADGET, as she inserts a cigarette.	It got to be about a quarter of eleven. . . I felt trapped, like the cigarette in the prongs of that contraption on her finger ...

PULL BACK TO:

NORMA AND GILLIS sitting on a couch in front of the cavernous fireplace. Norma holds out her cigarette to Gillis, who lights it.

Behind the Scenes

Scene C-9, The Tango

Billy and Gloria rehearse the dance scene between Norma and Joe.

SCENE C-6

NORMA
What a wonderful next year it's going to be. What fun we're going to have. I'll fill the pool for you. Or I'll open my house in Malibu, and you can have the whole ocean. Or I'll buy you a boat and we'll sail to Hawaii.

GILLIS
Stop it. You aren't going to buy me anything more.

NORMA
Don't be silly.
(She reaches under a pillow of the couch and brings out a leather box)
Here. I was going to give it to you at midnight.

Gillis opens the box. It contains a matched gold cigarette case and lighter.

NORMA
Read what's inside.

Gillis snaps open the case. Engraved inside the cover is: TO JOE FROM NORMA, and two bars of music.

GILLIS
What are the notes?

NORMA
"Mad about the boy."

GILLIS
Norma, I can't take it. You've bought me enough.

NORMA
Shut up. I'm rich. I'm richer than all this new Hollywood trash. I've got a million dollars.

GILLIS
Keep it.

NORMA
I own three blocks downtown. I have oil in Bakersfield -- pumping, pumping, pumping. What's it for but to buy us anything we want.

SCENE C-9

Gillis: Norma, I can't take it. You've bought me enough.
Norma: Shut up. I'm rich. I'm richer than all this
new Hollywood trash. I've got a million dollars.
Gillis: Keep it.

GILLIS
Cut out that us business.

He rises.

NORMA
What's the matter with you?

GILLIS
What right do you have to take me for granted?

NORMA
What right? Do you want me to tell you?

GILLIS
Has it ever occurred that I may have a life of my own? That there may be some girl I'm crazy about?

NORMA
Who? Some car hop, or a dress extra?

SCENE C-9

11454-22

11454-297

GILLIS
Why not? What I'm trying to say is that I'm all wrong for you. You want a Valentino -- somebody with polo ponies -- a big shot --

NORMA
(Getting up slowly)
What you're trying to say is that you don't want me to love you. Is that it?

Gillis doesn't answer. Norma slaps his face and rushes from the room and upstairs.

Gillis stands paralyzed, the slap burning his cheek.

C-10 THE TOP OF THE STAIRCASE AND CORRIDOR

Norma rushes up the last few steps, down the corridor and into her bedroom, banging the door. MOVE THE CAMERA toward the closed door, centering on the gouged-out lock.

C-11 GILLIS, IN THE BIG ROOM

He still stands motionless. He glances around furtively, to see if his humiliation has been observed.

C-12 THE ORCHESTRA

The musicians are playing away. They have turned their eyes away from Gillis rather too ostentatiously for comfort.

C-13 GILLIS

His eyes move over toward

C-14 MAX

He is subtler than the musicians. He appears very busy at the buffet, putting empty bottles and used glasses on a tray. He walks across the room with them.

3-22-49

SCENE C-9

C-15 GILLIS

He starts slowly out. As he does so his long gold key chain catches on a carved ornament of the sofa and holds him for a second of additional embarrassment. He yanks it loose and walks with as much nonchalance as he can muster to

C-16 THE HALL

Crossing towards the coat closet, Gillis throws a look upstairs. Then he pulls the Vicuna coat from its hanger and slips into it as he crosses to the entrance door. He opens the door on the darkness of the courtyard.

C-17 EXT. DESMOND HOUSE (NIGHT - RAIN)

Gillis shuts the door. He takes a few steps forward, then stands for a while breathing deep. The rain is balm to that cheek where the slap still burns. He walks forward with a great sense of relief.

GILLIS' VOICE

I didn't know where I was going. I just had to get out of there. I had to be with people my own age. I had to hear somebody laugh again. I thought of Artie Green. There was bound to be a New Year's shindig going on in his apartment down on Las Palmas -- the hock shop set -- not a job in the room, but lots of fun on the cuff.

C-18 DRIVEWAY LEADING TO SUNSET BOULEVARD

Gillis walks to the street, which is dark and empty. He starts down Sunset in an Easterly direction. A car passes. He tries to thumb a ride, without success. However, the second car, a florist's delivery wagon, stops. Gillis jumps in and the car drives off.

DISSOLVE TO:

SCENE C-19

C-19 ARTIE GREEN'S APARTMENT

It is the most modest one-room affair, jam-packed with young people flowing over into the miniature bathroom and the microscopic kitchenette. The only drink being served is punch from a pressed-glass bowl -- but everybody is having a hell of a time. Most of the men are in slacks and sweaters, and only a few of the girls in something that vaguely suggests party dress.

Abe Burroughs sits at a small, guest-festooned piano and sings Tokio Rose. By the door, a group of young men and girls respond to the song by singing Rinso White or Dentyne Chewing Gum or something similar, in the manner of a Bach choral. Artie Green, a dark haired, pleasant-looking guy in his late twenties, is conducting with the ladle from the punch bowl.

The door behind some of the singers is pushed open, jostling them out of their places. In comes Gillis, his hair and face wet, the collar of his Vicuna coat turned up. Artie stops conducting, but the commercial goes right on.

ARTIE
Well, what do you know! Joe Gillis!

GILLIS
Hi, Artie.

ARTIE
Where have you been keeping that gorgeous face of yours?

GILLIS
In a deep freeze.

ARTIE
I almost reported you to the Bureau of Missing Persons.
(To the company)
Fans, you all know Joe Gillis, the well-known screen writer, opium smuggler and Black Dahlia suspect.

Gillis greets some of the kids by name as he and Artie push their way into the room.

ARTIE
Give me your coat.

GILLIS
Let it ride for a while.

ARTIE
You're going to stay, aren't you?

SCENE C-19

Artie: Fans, you all know Joe Gillis,
the well-known screen writer, opium smuggler,
and Black Dahlia suspect.

GILLIS
That was the general idea.

ARTIE
Come on.

Artie starts peeling the coat off Gillis. Its texture takes his breath away.

ARTIE
What is this -- mink?

He has taken the coat. He looks at Gillis standing there in tails.

ARTIE
Judas H. Priest, who did you borrow that from? Adolphe Menjou?

GILLIS
Close, but no cigar.

Gillis stands embarrassed while Artie rolls up the Vicuna coat and tucks it above the books on a bookshelf.

ARTIE
Say, you're not really smuggling opium these days, are you?

GILLIS
Where's the bar?

The two make their way toward the punch bowl. It's a little like running the gauntlet for Gillis. There are whistles and stares of astonishment at his tails. When they reach the punch bowl, Artie picks up a half-filled glass and fills it.

GILLIS
Good party.

ARTIE
The greatest. They call me the Elsa Maxwell of the assistant directors.
(To some guests who are dipping their empty cups into the punch bowl)
Hey, easy on the punch bowl. Budget only calls for three drinks per extra. Fake the rest.

GILLIS
Listen, Artie, can I stick around here for a while?

ARTIE
Sure, this'll go on all night.

GILLIS
I mean, could you put me up for
a couple of weeks?

ARTIE
It just so happens we have a
vacancy on the couch.

GILLIS
I'll take it.

ARTIE
I'll have the bell-hop take care
of your luggage.

He runs his finger across the decollete back of a girl standing in a group next them.

ARTIE
Just register here.

The girl turns around. She is Betty Schaefer.

BETTY
Hello, Mr. Gillis.

ARTIE
You know each other?

Gillis looks at her a little puzzled.

BETTY
Let me help you. Betty Schaefer,
Sheldrake's office.

GILLIS
Sure. Bases Loaded.

ARTIE
Wait a minute. This is the woman
I love. What's going on? Who
was loaded?

GILLIS
Don't worry. She's just a fan
for my literary output.

BETTY
(to Artie)
Hurt feelings department.

SCENE C-19

Betty: I've been hoping to run into you.
Gillis: What for? To recover that knife you stuck in my back?

GILLIS
About that luggage. Where's the phone?

ARTIE
Over by the Rainbow Room.

Gillis squeezes his way through groups of people to the telephone, which is next to an open door leading to the bathroom. The phone is busy. A girl sits listening to it, giggling wildly. Another girl beside her is laughing too. They are apparently sharing a conversation with some man on the other end of the wire. The telephone passes from hand to hand. Gillis watches impatiently, then

GILLIS
When you're through with that thing, can I have it?

The girl just nods, going on with her chattering. Gillis stands waiting, and Betty Schaefer comes up with his glass.

BETTY
You forgot this.

GILLIS
Thanks.

BETTY
I've been hoping to run into you.

GILLIS
What for? To recover that knife you stuck in my back?

BETTY
I felt a little guilty, so I got out some of your old stories.

GILLIS
Why, you sweet kid.

BETTY
There's one called....Window... something with a window.

GILLIS
Dark Windows. How did you like it?

BETTY
I didn't.

GILLIS
Thank you.

BETTY
Except for about six pages. You've got a flashback there ...

There is too much racket for her.

BETTY
Is there someplace we can talk?

GILLIS
How about the Rainbow Room?

They squeeze their way towards the bathroom, past Artie.

ARTIE
I said you could have my couch. I didn't say you could have my girl.

BETTY
This is shop talk.

She and Gillis go through the open door into

C-20 ARTIE'S BATHROOM

It's a little less noisy, although there are some guests there, chatting and having fun. Betty and Gillis sit down on the edge of the tub.

GILLIS
Now if I got you correctly, there was a short stretch of my fiction you found worthy of notice.

BETTY
The flashback in the courtroom, when she tells about being a school teacher.

GILLIS
I had a teacher like that once.

BETTY
Maybe that's why it's good. It's true, it's moving. Now why don't you use that character...

GILLIS
Who wants true? Who wants moving?

BETTY
Drop that attitude. Here's something really worth while.

GILLIS
Want me to start right now? Maybe there's some paper around.

BETTY
I'm serious. I've got a few ideas.

GILLIS
I've got some ideas myself. One of them being this is New Year's Eve. How about living it up a little?

BETTY
As for instance?

GILLIS
Well....

BETTY
We could make some paper boats and have a regatta. Or should we just turn on the shower?

GILLIS
How about capturing the kitchen and barricading the door?

BETTY
Are you hungry?

GILLIS
Hungry? After twelve years in the Burmese jungle, I am starving, Lady Agatha -- starving for a white shoulder --

BETTY
Phillip, you're mad!

11454-74

One of the girls who was on the phone comes to the door.

GIRL
You can have the phone now.

GILLIS
(Paying no attention)
Thirsting for the coolness of your lips --

BETTY
No, Phillip, no. We must be strong. You're still wearing the uniform of the Coldstream Guards! Furthermore, you can have the phone now.

GILLIS
O.K.
(He gets up, starts out, turns)
I find I'm terribly afraid of losing you.

BETTY
You won't.
(She takes the glass out of his hand)
I'll get us a refill of this awful stuff.

GILLIS
You'll be waiting for me?

BETTY
With a wildly beating heart.

GILLIS
Life can be beautiful!

He leaves.

C-21 THE MAIN ROOM

Gillis squeezes himself through some guests to the phone. He has to stand in a cramped position, holding the instrument close to him as he dials a number.

GILLIS
Max? This is Mr. Gillis. I want you to do me a favor.

Scene C-20, Artie's Bathroom

Filming the party girls breaking up William Holden and Nancy Olson's mock love scene in the bathroom.

Behind the Scenes

Scenes C-23 to C-27, The Phone Call

Billy Wilder directs William Holden's reaction to Joe finding out that Norma has tried to commit suicide.

C-22 NORMA DESMOND HOUSE

Max is at the phone, in the lower hall.

MAX
I am sorry, Mr. Gillis.
I cannot talk now.

C-23 GILLIS ON THE PHONE

GILLIS
Yes you can. I want you to get my old suitcase and I want you to throw in my old clothes -- the ones I came with, and my typewriter. I'll have somebody pick them up.

C-24 MAX AT THE PHONE

MAX
I have no time to talk. The doctor is here.

C-25 GILLIS ON THE PHONE

GILLIS
What doctor? What's going on?

C-26 MAX ON THE PHONE

MAX
She got the razor from your room. She cut her wrists.

Max hangs up, moves toward the staircase.

C-27 GILLIS AT THE PHONE

GILLIS
Max! Max!

He hangs up the dead receiver, stands numb with shock. Betty elbows her way up to him, carrying the two punch glasses filled again.

BETTY
I just got the recipe: take two packages of cough drops, dissolve in one gallon of lukewarm grape juice --

Gillis looks up at her. Without a word he pushes her aside so that she spills the drink. He makes his way through the guests to the Vicuna coat, pulls it from the shelf, some books tumbling with it, and rushes towards the door and out. Betty stands looking after him, completely bewildered.

DISSOLVE TO:

C-28 EXT. DESMOND HOUSE - (NIGHT, RAIN)

The doctor's car is parked in the driveway. A taxi pulls up. Gillis, in his Vicuna coat now, jumps out, throws a couple of dollars to the driver and runs toward the house.

C-28a DOORWAY, NORMA DESMOND HOUSE

Max is opening the door to let out the doctor, a professional looking man carrying a black bag. Gillis runs into the SHOT.

GILLIS
How is she?

MAX
She is upstairs.

Gillis starts to push past Max. Max grabs his arm.

MAX
Be careful. Do not race up the stairs. The musicians must not know what has happened.

Gillis goes into the house.

C-29 ENTRANCE HALL AND STAIRCASE

Gillis crosses the hall and starts up the stairs.

C-30 INT. NORMA DESMOND'S ROOM

Only one alabaster lamp lights the big, cold room. On the bed lies Norma in her evening dress. She is white as a sheet. Her wrists are bandaged. Her eyes are wide open, staring at the ceiling. One of her shoes has half slipped off her foot. The other is on. Gillis opens the door and stands there for a second. Then he slowly moves to the foot of the bed. He takes the shoes from her feet and puts them on the floor.

SCENE C-30

11454-82

Scene C-30,
Norma's Bedroom

above: Wilder first directs Swanson in the pivotal scene between Norma and Joe.
opposite: Wilder shows Holden his blocking for the scene.

11454-2/47

SCENE C-30

NORMA
Go away.

GILLIS
What kind of a silly thing was that to do?

NORMA
To fall in love with you -- that was the idiotic thing.

GILLIS
It sure would have made attractive headlines: Great Star Kills Herself for Unknown Writer.

NORMA
Great stars have great pride.

She puts one bandaged forearm over her eyes, sobbing. Gillis walks slowly over to the mantelpiece, stands there for a while.

NORMA
Go away. Go to that girl of yours.

GILLIS
Look, I was making that up because I thought the whole thing was a mistake. I didn't want to hurt you. You've been good to me. You're the only person in this stinking town that has been good to me.

NORMA
Why don't you just say thank you and go, go, go --

GILLIS
Not until you promise to act like a sensible human being.

NORMA
I'll do it again, I'll do it again, I'll do it again!

Gillis stands looking at her helplessly.

C-31 LIVING ROOM, THE DESMOND HOUSE

The candles burned down, the orchestra playing to the emptiness. The orchestra leader looks at his watch, rises, silences the orchestra, then starts them in on Auld Lang Syne.

C-32 INT. NORMA'S ROOM

Gillis still stands. Norma lies on the bed, arms over her eyes, sobbing.

GILLIS
Happy New Year.

Norma continues to sob. Gillis goes to the bed, puts his arms on her shoulders and turns her around.

GILLIS
Happy New Year.

Norma looks at him, tears in her eyes. Slowly she enfolds him in her bandaged arms.

NORMA
Happy New Year, darling.

She kisses him.

DISSOLVE

END OF SEQUENCE "C"

Scenes C-30 to C-32, Norma's bedroom

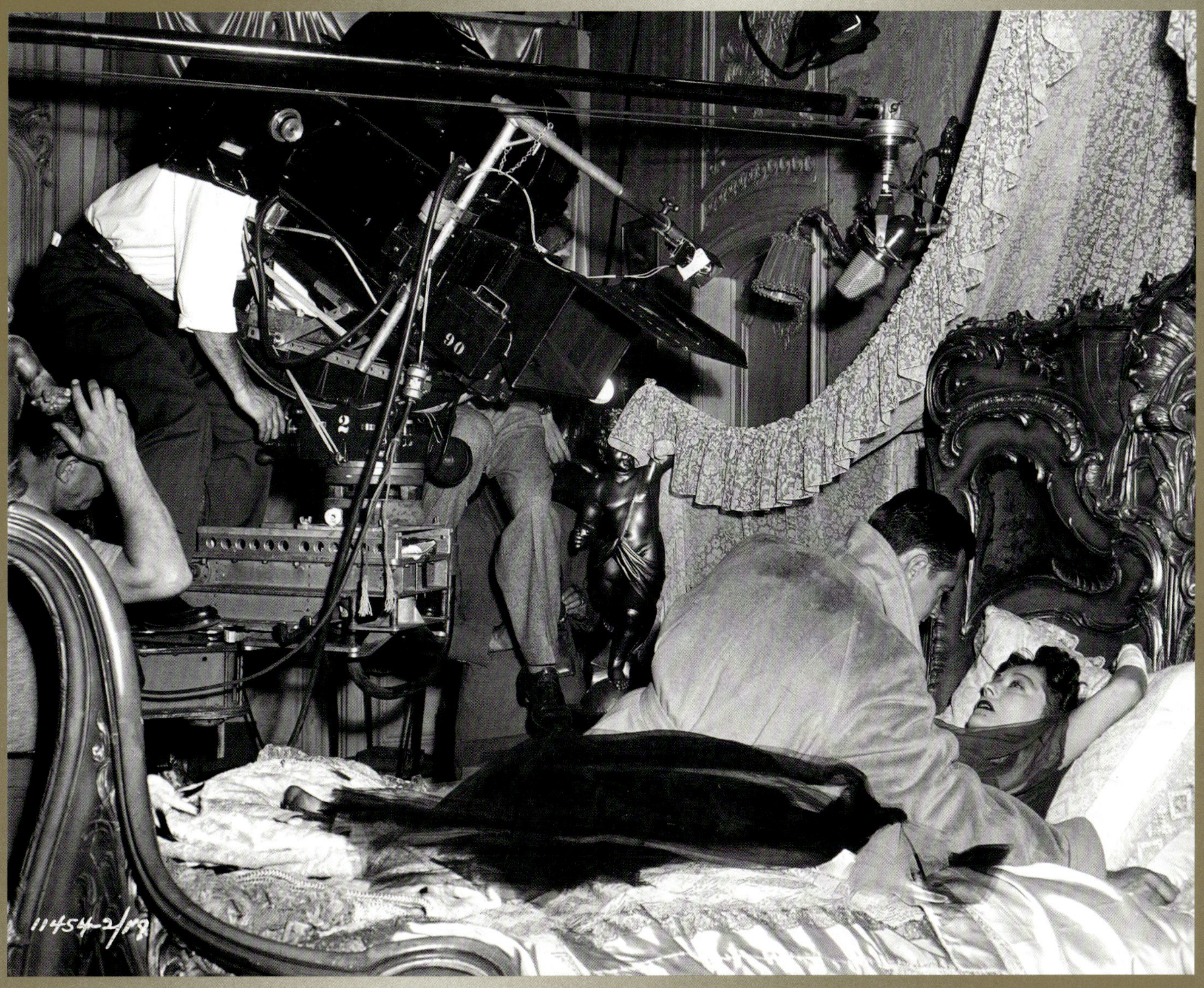

above: Wilder (far left) watches as cinematographer John F. Seitz gets the close-up of Holden and Swanson.

following pages: Wilder sets up the camera position for the close-up.

4-30-49 1st Change SUNSET BOULEVARD P.11454
65.

SEQUENCE "D"

DISSOLVE IN ON:

D-1 PATIO, NORMA DESMOND'S HOUSE
(A SUNNY DAY)

The garden is in somewhat better shape. The old house looks less unkempt. The pool is filled. Lying on a rubber mattress in the middle of it is Gillis, in bathing trunks. He is tanned and relaxed. Norma sits on a wicker chaise longue, her face shielded by an enormous straw hat, her eyes by dark glasses. She has been studying a typewritten letter.

GILLIS' VOICE
Come April, she had the pool filled up for me. We had finished that script of hers, such as it was...I wasn't a writer any more. I was drifting through a blurry novocaine existence. Pampered and spoiled and watched over as if I were some kind of a sickly Persian prince.

From the house comes the sounds of Bach rendered on the organ. Over it, the ringing of a phone.

NORMA
Shouldn't you be getting out of the water, darling? The masseur will be here any minute.

GILLIS
Yes, dear.

Lackadaisically, without changing his position, he starts paddling the raft towards the pool's edge. The phone rings again.

NORMA
Max! Max! Answer that phone!

D-1a HALLWAY, THE DESMOND HOUSE

Max comes from living room to the phone. He picks it up.

MAX
Hello ... Yes?

D-1b BETTY SCHAEFER, AT THE PHONE ON HER DESK IN THE READERS' DEPARTMENT

BETTY
Is this Crestview 5-1733? ... I'm sorry to bother you again, but I've confirmed the number. I must speak to Mr. Gillis.

Scene D-1, The Patio

Filming Norma and Joe poolside meant a somewhat precarious setup for the cameramen.

1454-28

D-1c MAX, AT THE PHONE

MAX
He is not here.

D-1d BETTY ON THE PHONE

BETTY
Where can I reach him? Maybe somebody else in the house could tell me.

D-1e MAX ON THE PHONE

MAX
Nobody here can give you any information. You will please not call again.

He hangs up. From off comes:

NORMA'S VOICE
Who was it, Max? What is it?

D-1f PATIO - DESMOND HOUSE

Max comes to the entrance door.

MAX
Nothing, Madame. Somebody inquiring about a stray dog. We must have a number very similar to the pound.

He starts to turn back.

NORMA
Wait a minute. I want you to get out the car. You're to take the script over to Paramount and deliver it to Mr. deMille in person.

MAX
Yes, Madame.

He goes into the house.

GILLIS
(Climbing out of the water)
You're really going to send it to deMille?

NORMA
This is the right day.
(Indicating the letter)

SCENE D-1F

NORMA (Cont'd)
The chart from my astrologer. She read deMille's horoscope. She read mine.

GILLIS
Did she read the script?

NORMA
DeMille is Leo. I'm Scorpio. Mars has been transitting Jupiter for weeks. Today is the day of greatest conjunction. Now turn around. Let me dry you.

She puts the towel around his shoulders and starts drying him.

GILLIS
I hope you realize, Norma, that scripts don't sell on astrologers' charts.

NORMA
I'm not just selling the script. I'm selling me. DeMille always said I was his greatest star.

GILLIS
When did he say it, Norma?

NORMA
So he said it quite a few years ago. So what? I never looked better in my life. Do you know why? Because I've never been as happy in my life.

She kisses him.

DISSOLVE TO:

D-2 INT. THE ISOTTA, DRIVING DOWN SUNSET ABOUT 8:30 IN THE EVENING

Max is driving. In the tonneau sit Norma, in a chinchilla wrap, and Gillis in his tuxedo. Norma is rummaging through her evening bag. She finds a cigarette case, opens it. It is empty.

GILLIS' VOICE
A few evenings later we were going to the house of one of the waxworks for some bridge. She'd taught me how to play bridge by then, just as she'd taught me some fancy tango steps, and what wine to drink with what fish.

NORMA
That idiot. He forgot to fill my cigarette case.

GILLIS
(Proffering his case)
Have one of mine.

NORMA
They're awful. They make me cough.

GILLIS
(Pushing open the glass partition, to Max)
Pull up at the drugstore, will you, Max.
(To Norma)
I'll get you some.

NORMA
You're a darling.

She takes a dollar bill from her purse and gives it to him.

D-3 EXT. SCHWAB'S DRUGSTORE

The car drives up and Gillis hurries into the store.

D-4 INT. SCHWAB'S DRUGSTORE

Business is still rather lively. There are about a dozen shoppers, and the soda counter is half filled. Gillis enters and steps to the tobacco counter.

GILLIS
(To the salesgirl)
Give me a pack of those Turkish cigarettes -- Melachrinos.

SCENE D-5

Betty: Sheldrake likes the angle about the teacher.
Gillis: What teacher?
Betty: Dark Windows. I got him all hopped up about it.

The girl opens the glass showcase to locate the fancy brand. From OFF comes

ARTIE'S VOICE
Stick 'em up, Gillis, or I'll let you have it!

Gillis turns.

D-5 AT THE SODA FOUNTAIN

Artie Green and Betty Schaefer sit having a sandwich and a milk shake. With his forefinger and a sound effect, Artie riddles Gillis' body. Gillis walks INTO THE SHOT.

GILLIS
Hello, Artie. Good evening, Miss Schaefer.

BETTY
(Excitedly)
You don't know how glad I am to see you!

ARTIE
Walking out on the mob. What's the big idea?

GILLIS
I'm sorry about New Year's. Would you believe me if I said I had to be with a sick friend?

ARTIE
Someone in the formal set, no doubt, with a ten-carat kidney stone.

BETTY
Stop it, Artie, will you?
(To Gillis)
Where have you been keeping yourself? I've got the most wonderful news for you.

GILLIS
I haven't been keeping myself at all. Not lately.

BETTY
I called your agent. I called the Screen Writers Guild. Finally your old apartment gave me some Crestview number. There was always somebody with an accent growling at me. You were not there. You were not to be spoken to. They never heard of you.

GILLIS
Is that so? What's the wonderful news?

BETTY
Sheldrake likes that angle about the teacher.

GILLIS
What teacher?

BETTY
Dark Windows. I got him all hopped up about it.

GILLIS
You did?

BETTY
He thinks it could be made into something.

GILLIS
Into what? A lampshade?

BETTY
Into something for Barbara Stanwyck. They have a commitment with Barbara Stanwyck.

ARTIE
Unless you'd rather have Sarah Bernhardt.

BETTY
This is on the level. Sheldrake really went for it.

GILLIS
O.K. Where's the cash?

BETTY
Where's the story? I bluffed it out with a few notions of my own. It's really just a springboard. It needs work.

GILLIS
I was afraid of that.

BETTY
I've got twenty pages of notes. I've got a pretty good character for the man.

ARTIE
Could you write in plenty of background action, so they'll need an extra assistant director?

BETTY
Shut up, Artie.
(To Gillis)
Now if we could sit down for two weeks and get a story.

GILLIS
Sorry, Miss Schaefer, but I've given up writing on spec.

BETTY
I tell you this is half sold.

GILLIS
As a matter of fact, I've given up writing altogether.

Max has appeared in the door.

MAX
Mr. Gillis, if you please.

GILLIS
Right with you.

Max leaves.

ARTIE
The accent! I've got it: this guy is in the pay of a foreign government. Get those studs. Get those cuff-links.

GILLIS
I've got to run along. Thanks anyway for your interest in my career.

BETTY
It's not <u>your</u> career -- it's mine. I kind of hoped to get in on this deal. I don't want to be a reader all my life. I want to write.

GILLIS
Sorry if I crossed you up.

BETTY
You sure have.

GILLIS
So long.

He leaves.

ARTIE
(Patting her hand)
Babe, it's like that producer says: In life, you've got to take the bitter with the sour.

D-6 THE ISOTTA, PARKED OUTSIDE

Gillis comes from Schwab's, gets into the car. Max takes off.

NORMA
What on earth, darling? It took you hours.

GILLIS
I ran into some people I knew.

NORMA
Where are my cigarettes?

GILLIS
Where are your...?

He realizes he's forgotten them, takes the dollar and hands it back to her.

GILLIS
Norma, you're smoking too much.

DISSOLVE TO:

D-7 LIVING ROOM, NORMA DESMOND'S HOUSE (EARLY AFTERNOON)

Start on a tiny parasol being twirled...Norma peeks out from one side of the parasol, a bandanna tied around her head with a rabbit's-ear bow. She bats her eyes, winks roguishly.

GILLIS' VOICE
Whenever she suspected I was getting bored, she would put on a live show for me: the Norma Desmond Follies. Her first number was always the Mack Sennett Bathing Beauty.

THE CAMERA PULLS BACK to reveal that Norma's black pyjama trousers are rolled up over her knees and her black stockings rolled down below them. The whole effect approximates a Mack Sennett bathing costume pretty effectively. She points at a leather pouf.

SCENE D-7

Gillis' Voice: Whenever she suspected I was getting bored, she would put on a live show for me: the Norma Desmond Follies. Her first number was always the Mack Sennett Bathing Beauty.

SCENE D-7

NORMA
This is a rock.

She climbs on it, pantomimes timidity, an attempted dive, then jumps off.

Gillis lolls on a couch, watching the performance, very bored.

NORMA
I can still see myself in the line: Bebe Daniels, Marie Prevost, Mabel Normand ... Mabel was always stepping on my feet ...What's the matter with you, darling? Why are you so glum?

GILLIS
(Lighting a cigarette with a match)
Nothing is the matter. I'm having a great time. Show me some more.

NORMA
(Taking the match)
All right. Give me this. I need it for a moustache. Now close your eyes.

She runs out of the picture. Gillis has closed his eyes. THE CAMERA MOVES to his face.

GILLIS' VOICE
Something was the matter, all right. I was thinking about that girl of Artie's, that Miss Schaefer. She was so like all us writers when we first hit Hollywood -- itching with ambition, panting to get your names up there: Screenplay by. Original Story by. Hmph! Audiences don't know somebody sits down and writes a picture. They think the actors make it up as they go along.

NORMA'S VOICE
Open your eyes.

Gillis opens his eyes.

Norma has equipped herself with a derby hat, a cane, and blacked in a small moustache. She goes into a little Chaplin routine. While she is doing it, the telephone rings. After a moment Max comes to the living room door.

MAX
Madame is wanted on the telephone.

NORMA
You know better than to interrupt me.

MAX
Paramount is calling.

NORMA
Who?

MAX
Paramount studios.

NORMA
(To Gillis)
Now, now do you believe me? I told you deMille would jump at it.

MAX
It is not Mr. deMille in person. It is someone by the name of Gordon Cole. He says it's very important.

NORMA
Certainly it's important. It's important enough for Mr. deMille to call me personally. The idea of having an assistant call me!

MAX
I myself was surprised at Mr. de Mille's manners.

NORMA
Say that I'm busy, and hang up.

MAX
Very good, Madam.

He bows and exits.

NORMA
How do you like that? We've made twelve pictures together. His greatest successes.

4-9-49

SCENE D-7

GILLIS
Maybe deMille is shooting.

NORMA
I know that trick! He wants to belittle me. He's trying to get my price down. I've waited twenty years for this call. Now Mr. deMille can wait till I'm good and ready.

DISSOLVE TO:

D-8 NORMA, IN THE TONNEAU OF THE LIMOUSINE, DRIVING DOWN MELROSE

She is in full makeup, with a veil, a daring hat, a suit so stunning only she would venture to wear it. THE CAMERA PULLS BACK. Beside her sits Gillis in the glen plaid suit. Max is driving.

GILLIS' VOICE
About three days later she was good and ready. Incredible as it may seem, there had been some more of those calls from Paramount. So she put on about half a pound of makeup, fixed it up with a veil, and set forth to see deMille in person.

Norma is examining her face in the mirror of her vanity. Max, while driving, sees her in the rear view mirror.

MAX
If you will pardon me, Madame. The shadow over the left eye is not quite balanced.

NORMA
Thank you, Max.

With a handkerchief, she corrects it.

D-9 MAIN GATE, EXT. PARAMOUNT STUDIO

The car drives down Bronson and stops smack in front of the iron gate. A young policeman is talking to an extra; an old policeman sits reading a newspaper. Max sounds the horn impatiently.

YOUNG POLICEMAN
Hold that noise!

MAX
To see Mr. deMille. Open the gate.

SCENE D-9

YOUNG POLICEMAN
Mr. deMille is shooting. You got an appointment?

MAX
No appointment is necessary. I am bringing Norma Desmond.

YOUNG POLICEMAN
Norma Who?

Norma has rolled down the window on her side. She calls to the old policeman.

NORMA
Jonesy! Come here, Jonesy!

OLD POLICEMAN
Yeah?
(He comes forward slowly)
Why, if it isn't Miss Desmond! How have you been, Miss Desmond?

NORMA
Fine, Jonesy. Now open that gate.

OLD POLICEMAN
Sure, Miss Desmond.
(To the young policeman)
Come on, Mac.

YOUNG POLICEMAN
They can't drive on the lot without a pass.

OLD POLICEMAN
Miss Desmond can. Come on.

They fling open the gate.

OLD POLICEMAN
(As the car drives through)
Stage eighteen, Miss Desmond.

NORMA
Thank you, Jonesy. And teach your friend some manners. Tell him without me he wouldn't have any job, because without me there wouldn't be any Paramount Studio.
(To Max)
Go on.

D-9, The Paramount Gate

Coming full circle: shooting the Paramount lot scene on the Paramount lot, right inside the famous arch.

11454-21

They drive through the gates. The old policeman goes to wall phone beside the gate, dials a number.

OLD POLICEMAN
(Into phone)
Norma Desmond coming in to see Mr. deMille.

D-10 STATE 18

A scene from SAMSON AND DELILAH is being rehearsed in the background. The usual turbulent activity surrounds it: extras, makeup men, grips, assistants, etc., etc. In the dim foreground a stage hand is answering a stand telephone. He puts down the phone and moves (CAMERA WITH HIM) to a second assistant.

STAGE HAND
Norma Desmond is coming to see Mr. deMille.

The second assistant walks (CAMERA WITH HIM) to the first assistant.

2nd ASSISTANT
Norma Desmond coming in to see Mr. deMille.

The first assistant (CAMERA WITH HIM) hurries to the set. Sitting with his back toward us is C.B. himself. He is rehearsing a scene with Hedy Lamarr.

1st ASSISTANT
Norma Desmond is coming in to see you, Mr. deMille.

C. B. turns his head.

DEMILLE
Norma Desmond?

1st ASSISTANT
She must be a million years old.

DE MILLE
I hate to think where that puts me. I could be her father.

1ST ASSISTANT
I'm terribly sorry, Mr. deMille.

By this time deMille is on his feet.

DE MILLE
It must be about that appalling script of hers. What can I say to her? What can I say?

1ST ASSISTANT
I could give her the brush.

DE MILLE
Nobody gives Norma Desmond the brush.
(To the set)
Hold everything.

He starts towards the door of the stage, the assistant following him.

D-11 EXT. STAGE 18

Norma's limousine drives up. Max dismounts and opens the door.

NORMA
(Taking Gillis' hand)
Don't you want to come along, darling?

GILLIS
I don't think so. It's your script. It's your show. Good luck.

NORMA
Thank you, darling.

She presses his hand against her cheek, descends from the car and walks toward --

Behind the Scenes

Scene D-10, Stage 18

The set behind the set: filming DeMille's reaction at his assistant director telling him Norma has arrived.

C.B.DE MILLE

D-12 THE DOOR OF STAGE 18

The first assistant is holding it open. In the doorway stands Mr. deMille. Seeing Norma, he stretches out his arms.

DE MILLE
Hello, young fellow.

NORMA
Hello, Mr. deMille.

She has reached him. They embrace.

NORMA
Last time I saw you was someplace very gay. I remember waving to you. I was dancing on a table.

DE MILLE
Lots of people were. Lindbergh had just landed in Paris. Come on in.

He leads her into

D-13 STAGE 18

During the ensuing dialogue, Mr. deMille walks Norma towards the set.

DE MILLE
Norma, I want to apologize for not calling you.

NORMA
You'd better. I'm very angry.

DE MILLE
I'm pretty busy, as you can see...

NORMA
That's no excuse. You read the script, didn't you?

DE MILLE
Yes, I did.

NORMA
Then you could have picked up the phone yourself instead of leaving it to one of your assistants.

DE MILLE
What assistant?

SCENE D-12

Norma: Last time I saw you was someplace very gay.
I remember waving to you. I was dancing on a table.
DeMille: Lots of people were. Lindbergh had just landed in Paris.

Behind the Scenes

Unscripted scene

Wilder sets up the microphone that will brush past Norma as a reminder of how things have changed on set. This bit is not in the final shooting script; it takes the place of Norma seeing a chair that belongs to DeMille's new star, Hedy Lamarr.

NORMA
Don't play innocent. Somebody named Gordon Cole.

DE MILLE
Gordon Cole?

NORMA
And if you hadn't been pretty darned interested in that script, he wouldn't have tried to get me on the phone ten times.

DE MILLE
Gordon Cole... Look, Norma, I'm in the middle of a rehearsal.
(Indicating his own chair)
Make yourself comfortable.

He walks onto the set, accompanied by his assistants.

DE MILLE
(Sotto voce, to his first assistant)
Get me Gordon Cole on the phone.

Meanwhile, Norma starts to sit, sees the name MISS LAMARR on the chair and with a look of distaste changes and sits on the one marked C.B. DE MILLE. From somewhere comes

A VOICE
Hey, Miss Desmond! Miss Desmond!

She looks around her.

VOICE
Up here!

Norma looks up at the scaffolding.

On the scaffold stands one of the electricians, next to his light.

ELECTRICIAN
It's me! It's Hog-eye!

Norma waves at him.

NORMA
Hello.

Hog-eye points his light at her.

HOG-EYE
Let's get a look at you.

The beam of the lamp moves toward Norma. It hits her. She sits bathed in light. A couple of old costume extras recognize her.

EXTRAS
Say, it's Norma!
Norma Desmond!

They rush over and start wringing her hand. Into the shot comes a middle-aged hairdresser.

HAIRDRESSER
Hello, Miss Desmond. It's Bessie.

Some elderly electricians and stagehands move in.

D-14 ANOTHER PART OF THE STAGE

The first assistant brings the portable phone to deMille. DeMille lifts the receiver.

DE MILLE
Hello.

D-15 GORDON COLE'S OFFICE IN THE PROPERTY DEPARTMENT, GORDON COLE ON THE PHONE.

COLE
Prop Department. Gordon Cole speaking.

Filming Norma.

Actors Julia Faye (center) and Henry Wilcoxon (in the soldier uniform) are among the extras who greet Norma on the set.

11454-27

D-16 DE MILLE ON THE PHONE

DE MILLE
Cole, this is C. B. deMille. Have you been calling Norma Desmond?... What's it about?

D-17 GORDON COLE, ON THE PHONE

COLE
It's that car of hers -- an old Isotta-Fraschini. Her chauffeur drove it on the lot the other day. It looks just right for the Crosby picture. We want to rent it for a couple of weeks.

D-18 DE MILLE ON THE PHONE

DE MILLE
(Troubled)
Oh. Well, thank you.

He hangs up, walks back towards Norma. (CAMERA WITH HIM).

Norma stills sits in the shaft of light, surrounded by about a dozen people who have come up to pay court. DeMille gestures up to Hog-eye and the light shifts away. The people about Norma disperse slowly with various ad-libs.

DE MILLE
Well, Norma ...
(He sits down next to her)
I got hold of Gordon Cole.

Norma hasn't heard a word.

NORMA
Did you see them? Did you see how they came?

DE MILLE
You know, crazy things happen in this business. I hope you haven't lost your sense of humor ...

11454-119

11454-125

NORMA
(Ignoring him)
They were crying like little children. Why? Because the Queen is back. The Queen!

DE MILLE
Norma dear, all those telephone calls --

NORMA
It's all right. I've forgiven you. You like the script, that's what matters.

DE MILLE
It's got a lot of good things. Of course, it would be a very expensive picture...

NORMA
Who cares? Can't you see them standing at the box office? Lines that stretch for blocks!

DE MILLE
Look, Norma, is isn't entirely my decision. New York must be consulted.

NORMA
I'm not afraid. Ask any exhibitor in the country. I am not forgotten.

DE MILLE
Of course you're not, Norma.

NORMA
Let's get one thing straight, here and now. I don't work before ten in the morning, and never after four-thirty in the afternoon.

The first assistant has come up.

1st ASSISTANT
We're ready with the shot, Mr. deMille.

DE MILLE
You'll pardon me, Norma? Why don't you just sit and watch?
(He steps onto the set)
O.K. Here we go.

1st ASSISTANT
Roll 'em.

DE MILLE
Action!

The scene starts.

Behind the Scenes

Scene D-18, On the Set

DeMille, Wilder, and Swanson
chat between takes.

Scene D-18, On the Set

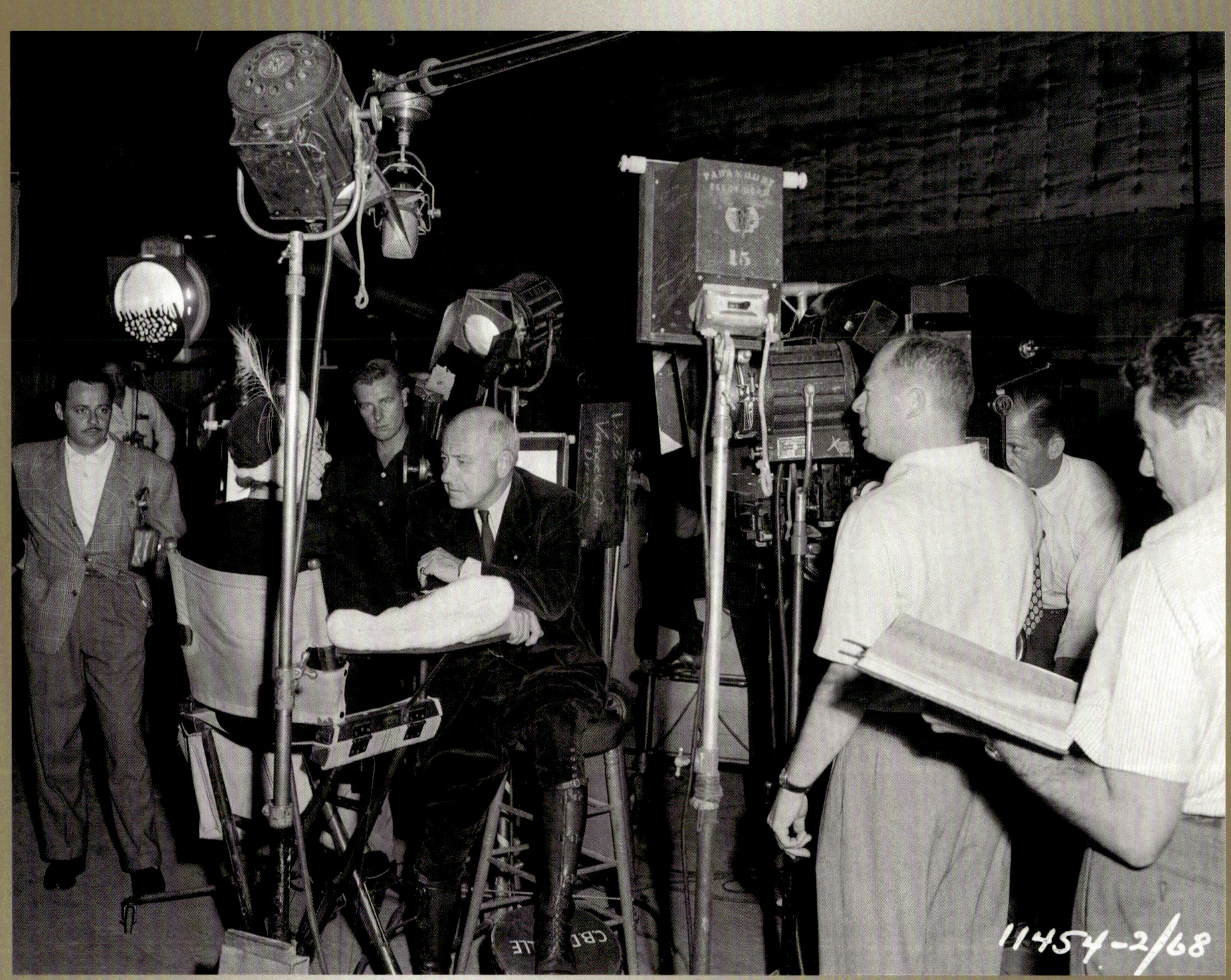

above, opposite: Same scene, different angles: filming DeMille trying (and failing) to break the news to Norma about Gordon Cole and the real reason for his call.

11454-122
William Farnum

SCENE D-19

Max: See where it says 'Readers Department'?
I remember my walls were covered with black patent leather . . .

D-19 THE ISOTTA, PARKED OUTSIDE STAGE 18

Max stands talking to Gillis, who is seated in the car.

MAX
(Pointing to the row of offices in the building opposite)
You see those offices there, Mr. Gillis? They used to be her dressing room. The whole row.

GILLIS
That didn't leave much for Wallace Reid.

MAX
He had a great big bungalow on wheels. I had the upstairs. See where it says 'Readers' Department'? I remember my walls were covered with black patent leather...

The words "Readers' Department" have registered on Gillis' mind. He gets out of the car.

GILLIS
I'll be with you in a minute.

He crosses the street towards the green staircase leading to the second floor.

Meanwhile, two prop men walking down the street come into the SHOT.

1ST PROP MAN
Hey, that's the comic car Cole was talking about!
(To Max)
Do you mind if we look inside?

MAX
Go away. Go away.

D-20 CUBICLE IN THE READERS' DEPARTMENT

Behind the desk sits Betty, typing the synopsis of a novel, a half-eaten apple marking her place. The door behind her opens and Gillis enters.

GILLIS
Just so you don't think I'm a complete swine -- if there's anything in Dark Windows you can use, take it. It's all yours.

BETTY
Well, for heaven's sake!

She moves the book and the apple aside and points at the free space on the desk.

BETTY
Have a chair.

Gillis sits on the desk.

GILLIS
I mean it. It's no good to me anyway. Help yourself.

BETTY
Why should you do that?

GILLIS
If you get a hundred thousand for it, you buy me a box of chocolate creams. If you get an Oscar, I get the left foot.

BETTY
You know, I'd take you up on that in a minute. I'm just not good enough to do it all by myself.

GILLIS
What about all those ideas you had?

BETTY
See if they make sense. To begin with, I think you should throw out all that psychological stuff -- exploring a killer's sick mind.

GILLIS
Psychopaths sell like hotcakes.

BETTY
This story is about teachers -- their threadbare lives, their struggles. Here are people doing the most important job in the world, and they have to worry about getting enough money to re-sole their shoes. To me it can be as exciting as any chase, any gunplay.

GILLIS
Check.

BETTY
Now I see her teaching day classes while he teaches night school. The first time they meet ...

From below comes the SOUND of the Isotta's horn.

GILLIS
Look, if you don't mind, I haven't got time to listen to the whole plot ...

BETTY
I'll make it short.

GILLIS
Sorry. It's your baby now.

BETTY
I'm not good enough to write it alone. We'll have to do it together.

GILLIS
I'm all tied up. I can't.

BETTY
Couldn't we work in the evenings? Six o'clock in the morning? This next month I'm completely at your disposal. Artie is out of town.

GILLIS
What has Artie to do with it.

BETTY
We're engaged.

GILLIS
Good for you. You've got yourself the best guy in town.

BETTY
I think so. They're on location in Arizona, shooting a Western. I'm free every evening, every week-end. If you want, we could work at your place.

GILLIS
It's just impossible.

BETTY
Nobody can be that busy.

There is another honk from down below.

GILLIS
Look, Betty, It can't be done. It's out.

BETTY
You're tough, all right.

GILLIS
You're on your own. Stop being chicken-hearted and write that story.

BETTY
Honest to goodness, I hate you.

GILLIS
(Turning in the open door)
And don't make it too dreary. How about this for a situation: she teaches daytimes. He teaches at night. Right? They don't even know each other, but they share the same room. It's cheaper that way. As a matter of fact, they sleep in the same bed -- in shifts, of course.

BETTY
Are you kidding? Because I think it's good.

GILLIS
So do I.

BETTY
Come on back. Let me show you where it fits in.

She reaches in a drawer for her notes on Dark Windows.

GILLIS
(At the door)
So long.

Betty picks up the apple and is about to throw it after him.

BETTY
Oh, you --

GILLIS
And here's a title: AN APPLE FOR THE TEACHER.

He ducks out quickly, slamming the door behind him. Betty looks after him, then angrily hurls the apple into the wastebasket.

D-21 STAIRCASE OUTSIDE READERS' DEPARTMENT

Max is rushing up the stairs toward the descending Gillis.

SCENE D-20

Betty: Couldn't we work in the evenings?
Six o'clock in the morning?
This next month I'm completely at your disposal.

11454-68

GILLIS
What's the matter, Max?

MAX
I just found out why all those telephone calls. It is not Miss Desmond they want. It is the car they want to rent.

GILLIS
What?

Max has seen something off.

MAX
Ssh...

With his head he indicates

D-22 THE ENTRANCE TO STAGE 18

The first assistant has opened the door. DeMille is showing Norma out.

DE MILLE
Goodbye, young fellow. We'll see what we can do.

NORMA
(embracing him)
I'm not worried. Everything will be fine. The old team together. Nothing can stop us.

She turns and walks out of the shot. De Mille stands for a second watching her, then turns to his assistant.

DE MILLE
Get Gordon Cole. Tell him to forget about her car. He can find another old car. I'll buy him five old cars, if necessary.

1ST ASSISTANT
Yes, Mr. De Mille.

They turn back into Stage 18.

4/11/49

SCENE D-21

D-23 THE ISOTTA

Gillis seated in the rear. Max is helping Norma in and putting the robe over her.

GILLIS
(Apprehensively)
How did it go?

NORMA
It couldn't have gone better. It's practically set. Of course, he has to finish this picture first, but mine will be his next.

There is an exchange of looks between Max and Gillis.

GILLIS
He must be quite a guy.

NORMA
He's a shrewd old fox. He can smell box office. Only I'm going to outfox him a little. This isn't going to be C. B. deMille's Salome. It's going to be Norma Desmond's Salome, a Norma Desmond Production, starring Norma Desmond...Home, Max.

MAX
Yes, Miss Desmond.

As he says the words, he and Gillis exchange a glance in the rear view mirror.

SLOW DISSOLVE:

END OF SEQUENCE "D"

11454-120

Behind the Scenes

Scene E-1, Norma's bedroom

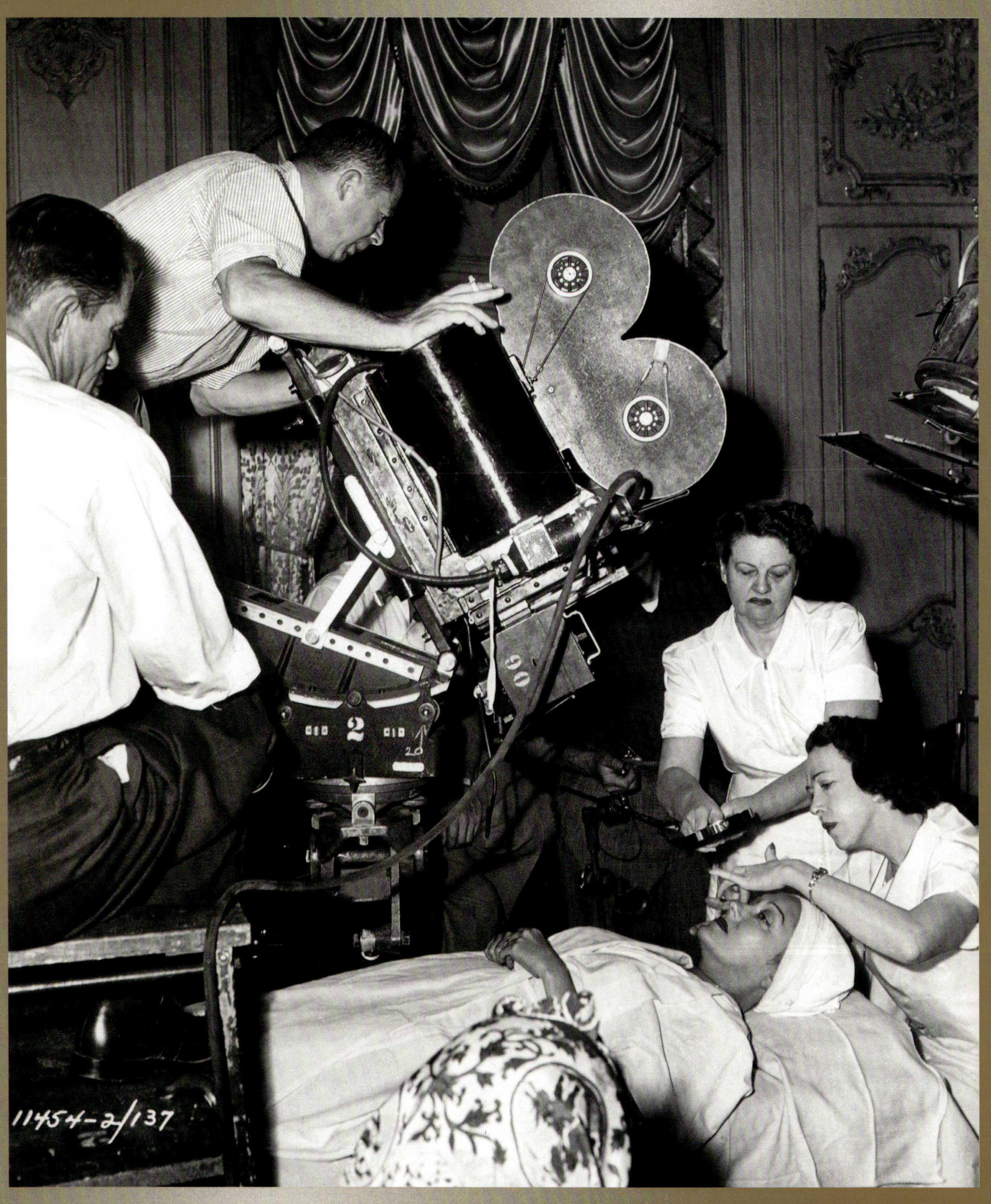

Wilder sets up the close-up for Norma's beauty treatment.

tv 1st Change SUNSET BOULEVARD 7-19-49 89.

SEQUENCE "E"

DISSOLVE IN ON:

E-1 CLOSEUP OF NORMA'S FACE

Absolutely no makeup. A hand with a strong small flashlight comes into the picture. The beam of the flashlight travels over the face, exploring it mercilessly. While the light is still on it, two pairs of creamed hands come into the shot and start to massage it.

GILLIS' VOICE
After that, an army of beauty experts invaded her house on Sunset Boulevard. She went through a merciless series of treatments, massages, sweat cabinets, mud baths, ice compresses, electric devices. She lived on vegetable juices and went to bed at nine. She was determined to be ready -- ready for those cameras that would never turn.

DISSOLVE TO:

E-2 A SHORT MONTAGE of various beauty treatments applied to Norma.

DISSOLVE TO:

E-3 NORMA BEFORE THE MIRROR IN HER BEDROOM

It is nine o'clock in the evening. She is in night gown and negligee and has put triangular patches on the saddle of her nose and at the outer corner of each eye. She is rubbing lotion on her hands.

She gets up and crosses to the door of Gillis' room and opens it a crack.

NORMA
Joe darling, are you there?

E-4 GILLIS' ROOM

It is dark except for a lamp over the chaise longue. Gillis lies on it, fully clothed, reading a book.

GILLIS
Yes, Norma.

Through the slit in the door there is a suggestion of Norma.

NORMA
Don't turn around. Keep your eyes on the book.

GILLIS
Yes, Norma.

Norma pushes the door open and comes in.

NORMA
I just came to say good night. I don't want you to see me -- I'm not very attractive.

GILLIS
Good night.

NORMA
I've lost half a pound since Tuesday.

GILLIS
Good.

NORMA
I was a little worried about the line of my throat. This woman has done wonders with it.

GILLIS
Good.

NORMA
You'd better get to bed yourself.

GILLIS
I think I'll read a little.

NORMA
You went out last night, didn't you, Joe?

GILLIS
Why do you say that?

NORMA
I just happen to know it. I had a nightmare and I screamed for you. You weren't here. Where were you?

GILLIS
I went for a walk.

5-17-49

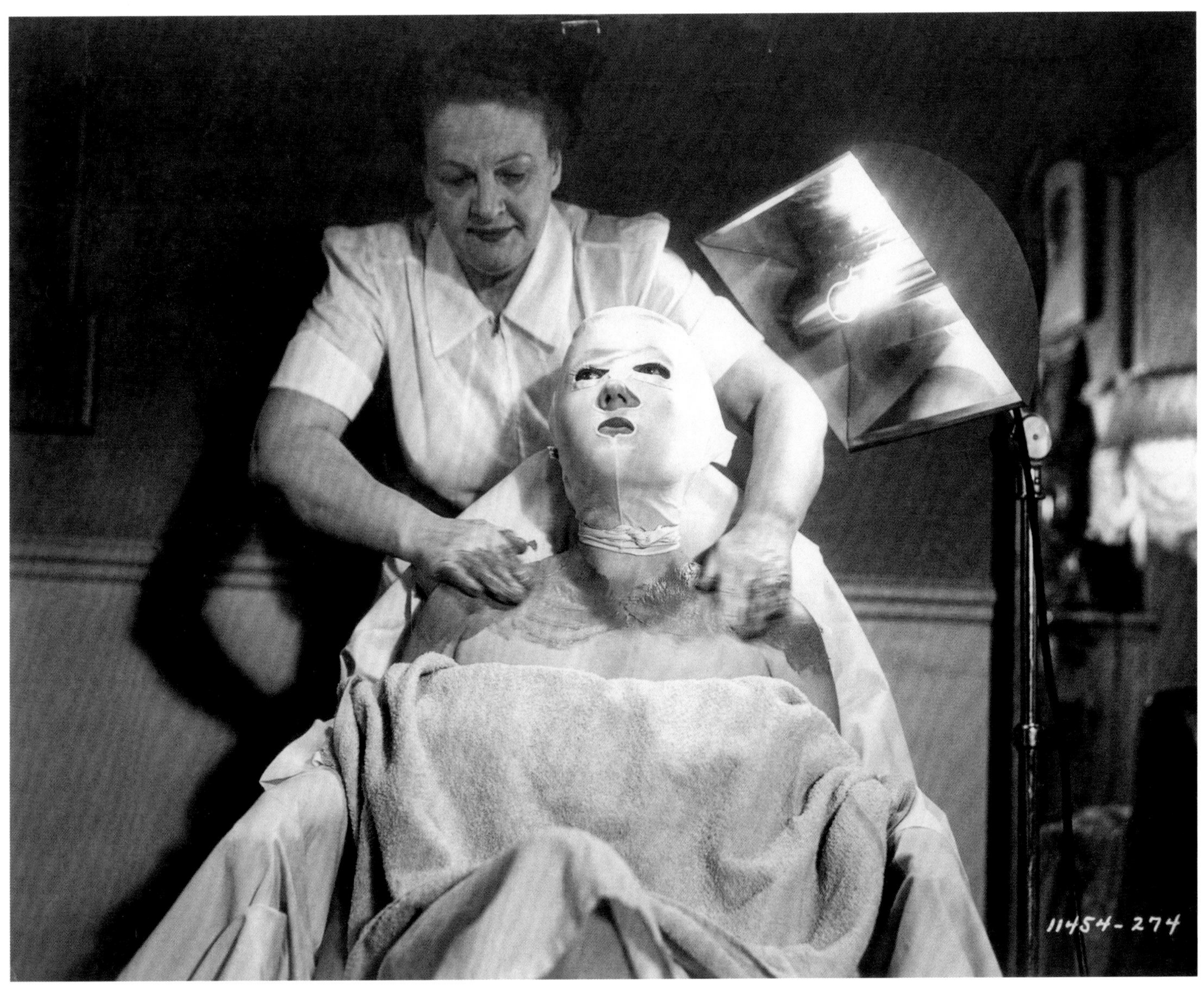

SCENE E-1

NORMA
No you didn't. You took the car.

GILLIS
All right, I drove to the beach. Norma, you don't want me to feel I'm locked up in this house?

NORMA
Of course not, Joe. It's just that I don't want to be left alone. Not now, while I'm under this terrible strain. My nerves are being torn apart. All I ask is for you to be a little patient and a little kind.

GILLIS
I haven't done anything, Norma.

NORMA
Of course you haven't. I wouldn't let you.

She bends and kisses the top of his head.

NORMA
Good night, my darling.

She goes into her room, shutting the door behind her.

Gillis puts his book down and looks at her door.

E-5 THE DOOR TO NORMA'S ROOM

The light can be seen through the gouged-out keyhole. It goes out.

DISSOLVE TO:

5-17-49

E-6 UPPER LANDING, STAIRWAY AND HALL BELOW (NIGHT)

Gillis, with his coat on by now, comes cautiously to the upper railing and looks down into the lighted hall below.

Max is just extinguishing the lights. Max exits in the direction of the living room.

After a moment Gillis starts silently down the stairs.

GILLIS' VOICE

Yes, I was playing hooky every evening along in there. It made me think of when I was twelve and used to sneak out on the folks to see a gangster picture. This time it wasn't to see a picture, it was to try and write one. That story of mine Betty Schaefer had dug up kept going through my head like a dozen locomotives...

E-7 LIVING ROOM

(Lighted only by the last flicker of a fire on the hearth). Max is putting a fire screen in front of the fire. He hears some steps and the creak of the main door being opened. He looks out and sees

E-7a THE MAIN DOOR

Gillis, in the moonlit porch, is closing the main door behind him.

E-8 LIVING ROOM

Max looks after Gillis, his face enigmatic as ever.

DISSOLVE TO:

E-9 GARAGE AND DRIVEWAY (MOONLIGHT)

Gillis comes into the shot, gets into the Isotta, drives it out of the garage and down the driveway to Sunset, as quietly as possible.

DISSOLVE TO:

SCENE E-10

E-10 READERS' OFFICE BUILDING
PARAMOUNT (NIGHT)

Start on a LONG SHOT. THE BOOM MOVES FORWARD to the only two lights. They are the door and window of Betty Schaefer's cubicle. Betty sits at the desk, typing. Gillis, his coat off, his shirt-sleeves rolled up, is pacing the floor, discussing the construction of a sentence. The discussion at a stalemate, Betty suggests some coffee. Gillis agrees. From the electric plate on the shelf beside her, Betty takes a glass coffee machine. Gillis seats himself in her chair and starts typing.

GILLIS' VOICE
So we'd started working on it, the two of us. Nights, when the studio was deserted, up in her little cubby-hole of an office.

Betty opens the door and comes out on the balcony to fill the coffee machine from the water cooler standing beside the door.

BETTY
I got the funniest letter from Artie. It's rained every day since they got to Arizona. They re-wrote the whole picture for rain and shot half of it. Now the sun is out. Nobody knows when they'll get back.

She moves back into the room.

GILLIS
Good.

BETTY
What's good about it? I miss him something fierce.

GILLIS
I mean this is good dialogue along in here. It'll play.

BETTY
It will?

GILLIS
Sure. Especially with lots of music underneath, drowning it out.

7-19-49

BETTY
Don't you sometimes hate yourself?

GILLIS
Constantly. No, in all seriousness, it's really good. It's fun writing again. I'm happy here, honest I am.

He resumes typing. Betty puts the water on. She picks up a pack of cigarettes on the desk, finds it's empty and throws it away, sees Gillis' open gold cigarette case and lighter on the table by the couch. Betty reaches for a cigarette. The inscription engraved inside the case catches her eye. It reads:

MAD ABOUT THE BOY --

Norma

BETTY
Who's Norma?

GILLIS
Who's who?

BETTY
I'm sorry. I don't usually read private cigarette cases.

GILLIS
Oh, that. It's from a friend of mine. A middle-aged lady, very foolish and very generous.

BETTY
I'll say. This is solid gold.

GILLIS
I gave her some advice on an idiotic script.

BETTY
It's that old familiar story? you help a timid little soul across a crowded street. She turns out to be a multimillionaire and leaves you all her money.

GILLIS
That's the trouble with you readers. You know all the plots. Now suppose you proof-read page ten while the water boils.

DISSILVE TO:

SCENE E-12

Betty: I was born just two blocks from this studio. Right on Lemon Grove Avenue. Father was head electrician here till he died. Mother still works in Wardrobe.
Gillis: Second generation, huh?
Betty: Third. Grandma did stunt work for Pearl White.

E-11 AN EMPTY STREET AT THE PARAMOUNT STUDIO (NIGHT)

Gillis and Betty are walking down it. From a stage where they are erecting a new set comes a great shaft of light. They stop at an apple-vending machine in the foreground, buy themselves a couple of apples and walk on.

GILLIS' VOICE
Sometimes when we got stuck we'd make a little tour of the drowsing lot, not talking much, just wandering down alleys between the sound stages, or through the sets they were getting ready for the next day's shooting. As a matter of fact, it was on one of those walks when she first told me about her nose ...

DISSOLVE TO:

E-12 PARAMOUNT'S NEW YORK STREET (NIGHT)

Betty and Gillis are walking down it, THE CAMERA AHEAD OF THEM.

BETTY
Look at this street. All cardboard, all hollow, all phoney. All done with mirrors. I like it better than any street in the world. Maybe because I used to play here when I was a kid.

GILLIS
What were you -- a child actress?

BETTY
I was born just two blocks from this studio. Right on Lemon Grove Avenue. Father was head electrician here till he died. Mother still works in Wardrobe.

GILLIS
Second generation, huh?

BETTY
Third. Grandma did stunt work for Pearl White. I come from a picture family. Naturally they took it for granted I was to become a great star. So I had ten years of dramatic lessons, diction, dancing. Then the studio made a test. Well, they didn't like my nose -- it slanted this way a little. I went to a doctor and had it fixed. They made more tests, and they were crazy about my nose -- only they didn't like my acting.

11454-148

SCENE E-12

Gillis: Three cheers for Betty Schaefer!
I will now kiss that nose of yours.
Betty: If you please.

GILLIS
(Examining her nose by the flame of his lighter)
Nice job.

BETTY
Should be. It cost three hundred dollars.

GILLIS
Saddest thing I ever heard.

BETTY
Not at all. It taught me a little sense. I got me a job in the mail room, worked up to the Stenographic. Now I'm a reader ...

GILLIS
Come clean, Betty. At night you weep for those lost closeups, those gala openings ...

BETTY
Not once. What's wrong with being on the other side of the cameras? It's really more fun.

GILLIS
Three cheers for Betty Schaefer! I will now kiss that nose of yours.

BETTY
If you please.

Gillis kisses her nose. As he stands there, his face close to hers --

GILLIS
May I say you smell real special.

BETTY
It must be my new shampoo.

GILLIS
That's no shampoo. It's more like a pile of freshly laundred handkerchiefs, like a brand new automobile. How old are you anyway?

BETTY
Twenty-two.

GILLIS
That's it. You smell of being twenty-two. And may I suggest that if we're ever to finish this story, you keep at least two feet away from me. And the first time you see me come any closer, I want you to take off a shoe and clunk me over the head with it. Now back to the typewriter.

They start walking in the direction of the office.

DISSOLVE TO:

E-13 THE GARAGE

Gillis gets out. From the seat next him he takes a batch of script, folds it and puts it in his pocket. He suddenly becomes aware that he is watched, turns. Max stands in the moonlight, evidently waiting for him.

GILLIS
What is it, Max? Want to wash the car, or are you doing a little spying in your off hours?

MAX
You must be very careful as you cross the patio. Madame may be watching.

GILLIS
How about my going up the kitchen stairs and undressing in the dark. Will that do it?

MAX
I'm not inquiring where Mr. Gillis goes every night ...

GILLIS
Why don't you? I'm writing a script and I'm going to finish it, no matter what.

MAX
It's just that I'm very worried about Madame.

7-19-49

GILLIS
Sure you are. And we're not helping her any, feeding her lies and more lies. Getting herself ready for a picture ... What happens when she finds out?

MAX
She never will. That is my job. It has been for a long time. You must understand I discovered her when she was eighteen. I made her a star. I cannot let her be destroyed.

GILLIS
You made her a star?

MAX
I directed all her early pictures. There were three young directors who showed promise in those days: D.W. Griffith, C.B. deMille, and Max von Mayerling.

GILLIS
And she's turned you into a servant.

MAX
It was I who asked to come back, humiliating as it may seem. I could have gone on with my career, only I found everything unendurable after she divorced me. You see, I was her first husband.

DISSOLVE TO:

E-14 NORMA DESMOND'S BEDROOM

One lamp lit. Norma, in a white negligee, with the patches on her face, is pacing up and down -- a small, tormented, pitiable woman. Finally she opens the door to:

E-15 GILLIS' ROOM (MOONLIGHT)

Gillis lies in bed asleep, Norma in the doorway.

7-19-49

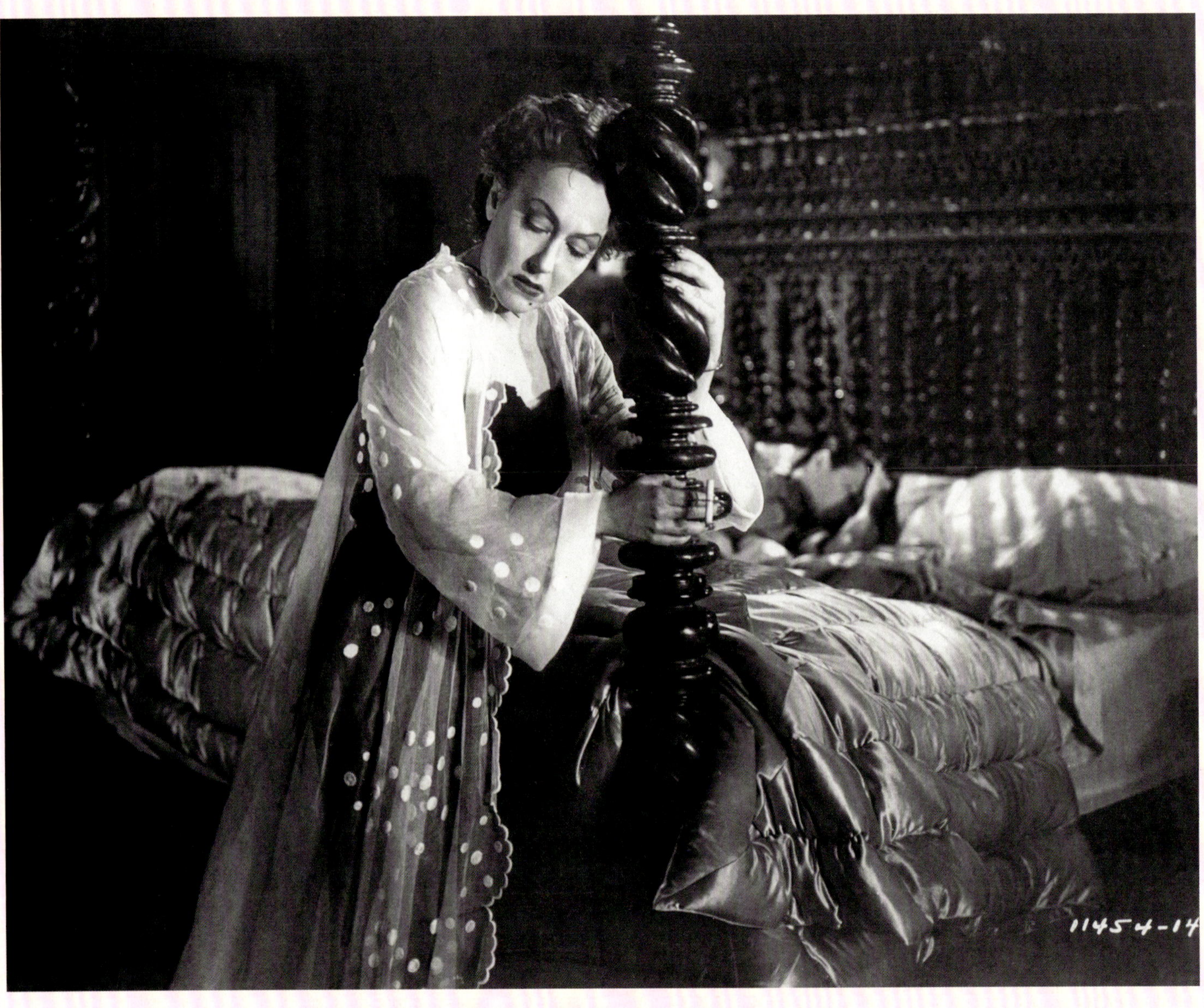

SCENE E-15

Norma: Where were you? Is it a woman?
I know it's a woman . . . Who is she? Oh Joe, why can't I ask you?

NORMA
You're here, Joe ... When did you come home? Where were you? Is it a woman? I know it's a woman ... Who is she? Oh Joe, why can't I ask you? I must know, I must!

Her eyes fall on Gillis' coat, which hangs over a chair. In a pocket is part of the script. Norma takes it out, looks at it. She can't see it in the moonlight. She hurries with it into:

E-16 NORMA'S BEDROOM

Carrying the script Norma goes to the lamp and looks at it. On the first page she sees something which confirms all her suspicions. It reads:

UNTITLED LOVE STORY
by
Joseph C. Gillis
and
Betty Schaefer

DISSOLVE:

E-17 BETTY'S CUBICLE (NIGHT)

Betty is typing. Gillis sits on the couch, proof-reading a scene. Betty stops typing and Gillis becomes aware of her eyes fixed on him.

GILLIS
Hey, what's the matter ... Betty, wake up!
(He whistles and catches her attention)
Why are you staring at me like that?

BETTY
Was I? I'm sorry.

GILLIS
What's wrong with you tonight? What is it, Betty?

BETTY
Something came up. I don't want to talk about it.

7-19-49

11454-6

GILLIS
Why not?

BETTY
I just don't.

GILLIS
What is it you've heard. Come on, let's have it.

Betty gets up.

GILLIS
Is it about me?

Betty doesn't answer, walks out on

E-18 THE BALCONY

She leans against a post, crying. Gillis comes out after her.

GILLIS
Betty, there's no use running out on it. Let's face it, whatever it is.

BETTY
It's nothing. I got a telegram from Artie.

GILLIS
From Artie. What's wrong?

BETTY
He wants me to come on to Arizona. He says it only costs two dollars to get married there. It would kind of save us a honeymoon.

GILLIS
Why don't you? We can finish the script by Thursday.

Betty stands crying silently.

GILLIS
Stop crying. You're getting married. That's what you've always wanted.

BETTY
I don't want it now.

7-19-49

SCENE E-18

GILLIS
Why not? Don't you love Artie?

BETTY
Of course I love him. I always will. I'm just not in love with him any more.

GILLIS
What happened?

BETTY
You did.

There is a moment's pause before he takes her in his arms. THE CAMERA MOVES AWAY.

DISSOLVE TO:

E-19 HALL AND STAIRCASE, DESMOND HOME (NIGHT)

Gillis enters, closes the door as quietly as he can, and goes up the stairs.

E-20 GILLIS' ROOM

He enters and turns on the light. He sinks down on the chaise longue, thinking. His eyes wander to the door of Norma's room. Through the gouged-out keyhole he sees the light.

GILLIS' VOICE
Well, there it was, right in the palm of my hand -- the future of Betty Schaefer, engaged to Artie Green, the nicest guy that ever lived. Ready to give him up for me. Me! She was a fool, and I loved her and I'd been a heel not to tell her. Maybe I'd never have to. Maybe I could get away with it. Away from Norma. Maybe I could wipe the whole nasty mess right out of my life.

From Norma's room comes the sound of a telephone being dialled. Gillis enters the shot and stands listening.

NORMA'S VOICE
Is this Gladstone 0858?

E-21 NORMA'S BEDROOM

Norma lies in bed, dialing a number. She has the beauty patches at the corners of her eyes and over her nose.

7-19-49

NORMA
Can I speak to Miss Betty Schaefer? She must be home by now.

E-22 A BEDROOM IN BETTY'S FLAT

Connie, a girl of Betty's age with whom she shares the flat, is on the phone. Betty, in a dressing-gown, comes from the bathroom, toothbrush in hand.

CONNIE
(Hand over mouthpiece)
Betty, here's that weird-sounding woman again.

BETTY
What is this anyway?
(Taking the phone)
This is Betty Schaefer.

E-23 NORMA AT THE PHONE

NORMA
Miss Schaefer, you must forgive me for calling you so late, but I really feel it's my duty. It's about Mr. Gillis. You do know Mr. Gillis? ...Exactly how much do you know about him? Do you know where he lives? Do you know how he lives? Do you know what he lives on?

E-24 BETTY AT THE PHONE

BETTY
Who are you? What do you want? What business is it of yours anyway?

E-25 NORMA ON THE PHONE

NORMA
Miss Schaefer, I'm trying to do you a favor. I'm trying to spare you a great deal of misery. Of course you may be too young to even suspect there are men of his sort ...

7-19-49

NORMA (Cont'd)
I don't know what he's told you, but he does not live with relatives, nor with friends, in the usual sense of the word. Ask him ... Ask him again.

During the latter part of her call, the doors from Gillis' room have been pushed open and Gillis has walked towards her. Suddenly Norma senses his presence and turns around. The telephone freezes in her hand. She tries to hang it up. Very calmly Gillis takes the receiver from her hand.

GILLIS
(Into phone)
That's right, Betty, ask me again. This is Joe.

E-26 BETTY ON THE PHONE

BETTY
Joe, where are you? What's this all about?

E-27 GILLIS ON THE PHONE

Norma beside him.

GILLIS
Or maybe it would be a better idea if you came over and saw it for yourself. The address is 10086 Sunset Boulevard.

He hangs up. Norma looks up at him as he crosses to the other end of the room and stands staring at her. The silence becomes unbearable.

NORMA
Don't hate me, Joe. I did it because I need you. I need you as I never needed you. Look at me. Look at my hands, look at my face, look under my eyes. How can I go back to work if I'm wasting away under this torment? You don't know what I've been through these last weeks. I got myself a revolver. You don't believe me, but I did, I did! I stood in front of that mirror, only I couldn't make myself. It wouldn't be

7-19-49

SCENE E-25

SCENE E-26

SCENE E-27

NORMA (Cont'd)
fair to all those people who are waiting to see me back on the screen. I can't disappoint them. Only, if I'm to work, I need sleep, I need quiet, I need you! Don't just stand there hating me! Shout at me, strike me! But don't hate me, Joe. Don't you hear me, Joe?

GILLIS
Yes, I hear you. And I wish you'd keep still so I can hear the doorbell when she rings it.

E-28 BETTY AND CONNIE, DRIVING IN A SMALL COUPE DOWN SUNSET BOULEVARD (NIGHT)

E-29 INT. COUPE

Connie is looking at the house numbers.

CONNIE
Here's ten thousand seventy-nine, Betty. It must be over there.

Betty turns the car into the driveway of Norma's place, stops at the entrance steps. Betty gets out.

CONNIE
Betty, let me come along with you. Please.

BETTY
No. I'll be all right.

She shuts the door of the car and goes up the steps.

E-30 NORMA'S BEDROOM

Norma lies on the bed. Gillis sits in a far corner of the room, motionless.

NORMA
(In a whimpering monotone)
I love you, Joe. I love you, Joe.
I love you, Joe. I love you, Joe.

There is the sound of footsteps below and the ringing of a doorbell. Gillis rises.

7-19-49

NORMA
What are you going to do, Joe?

Without a word, he leaves the room. Norma raises herself on the bed, reaching for a black negligee lying at the foot of it. As she does so, she dislodges her pillow a little, revealing a revolver hidden beneath it.

E-31 DOWNSTAIRS HALL, THE DESMOND HOUSE (DARK)

Max crosses the hall, putting on his alpaca jacket. He turns on the lights. Outside stands Betty. From the staircase comes -

GILLIS' VOICE
It's all right, Max. I'll take it.

MAX
Yes, sir.

He stands back as Gillis opens the door.

GILLIS
Hello, Betty.

BETTY
(On the threshold)
I don't know why I'm so scared, Joe. Is it something awful?

GILLIS
Come on in, Betty.

Betty enters. As he leads her into the living room, Gillis puts his arm around her shoulders.

GILLIS
Ever been in one of these old Hollywood palazzos? That's from when they were making eighteen thousand a week, and no taxes. Careful of these tiles, they're slippery. Valentino used to dance here.

BETTY
This is where you live?

GILLIS
You bet.

BETTY
Whose house is it?

7-19-49

SCENE E-38

Gillis: This is an enormous place. Eight master bedrooms.
A sunken tub in every bathroom. There's a bowling alley in the cellar.
It's lonely here, so she got herself a companion. A very simple set-up:
An older woman who is well-to-do. A younger man who is not doing too well . . .
Can you figure it out yourself?

They have reached

E-32 THE LIVING ROOM

Gillis leads Betty in.

GILLIS
Hers.

BETTY
Whose?

GILLIS
Just look around. There's a lot of her spread about. If you don't remember the face, you must have heard the name of Norma Desmond.

BETTY
That was Norma Desmond on the phone?

GILLIS
Want something to drink? There's always champagne on ice, and plenty of caviar.

BETTY
Why did she call me?

GILLIS
Jealous. Ever see so much junk? She had the ceiling brought from Portugal. Look at this.

He pulls the rope, showing the projection screen under the picture.

GILLIS
Her own movie theatre.

BETTY
I didn't come here to see a house. What about Norma Desmond?

GILLIS
I'm trying to tell you. This is an enormous place. Eight master bedrooms. A sunken tub in every bathroom. There's a bowling alley in the cellar. It's lonely here, so she got herself a companion. A very simple set-up: An older woman who is well-to-do. A younger man who is not doing too well ... Can you figure it out yourself?

7-19-49

BETTY
No.

GILLIS
All right. I'll give you a few more clues.

BETTY
No, no! I haven't heard any of this. I never got those telephone calls. I've never been in this house ... Get your things together. Let's get out of here.

GILLIS
All my things? All the eighteen suits, all the custom-made shoes and the eighteen dozen shirts, and the cuff-links and the platinum key-chains, and the cigarette cases?

BETTY
Come on, Joe.

GILLIS
Come on where? Back to a one-room apartment that I can't pay for? Back to a story that may sell and very possibly will not?

BETTY
If you love me, Joe.

GILLIS
Look, sweetie -- be practical. I've got a good thing here. A long-term contract with no options. I like it that way. Maybe it's not very admirable. Well, you and Artie can be admirable.

BETTY
Joe, I can't look at you any more.

GILLIS
Nobody asked you to.

Betty turns from him, to hide the fact that she is crying.

GILLIS
All right, baby. This way out.

He leads her in the direction of the door.

E-33 UPPER LANDING, DESMOND HOUSE

Sitting crouched behind the balustrade is Norma, peering down into

E-34 THE LOWER HALL

Betty and Gillis have reached the entrance door. Gillis opens it.

GILLIS
Good luck to you, Betty. You can finish that story on the way to Arizona. When you and Artie get back, if the two of you ever feel like a swim, here's the pool ...

He switches on the light.

E-35 THE PATIO

The lights go on in the pool, which shines brilliantly in the dark garden.

E-36 BETTY

She doesn't even look. Her eyes filled with tears, she runs down the entrance porch toward her car.

E-37 THE ENTRANCE HALL

Gillis looks after her, closes the door. From the upper landing comes the sound of soft sobbing. He looks up.

E-38 NORMA, ON THE UPPER LANDING

Gillis ascends the stairs.

NORMA
Thank you, Joe -- thank you, Joe.

She tries to take his hand to kiss it as he passes. He doesn't stop. Norma catches his coat. Gillis moves right on into his room. Norma lies on the floor looking after him. She crawls toward a console, pulls herself up by it, starts towards Gillis' door, passes a mirror, realizes how she looks, moves back to the mirror and takes the patches off her face and does a hasty job of removing the cream with her handkerchief, readjusts her expression to a poor travesty of a smile and goes to the door of Gillis' room.

SCENE E-34

11454-143

SCENE E-39

Norma: What are you doing, Joe?
What are you doing? You're not leaving me?
Gillis: Yes, I am, Norma.
Norma: No, you're not. (Calling) Max! Max!
Gillis: Max is a good idea. He can help with my luggage.

NORMA
May I come in? I've stopped crying. I'm all right again. Joe, tell me you're not cross -- tell me everything is just as it was, Joe.

She opens the door.

E-39 GILLIS' ROOM

In the foreground, open on the bed, is a half-packed suitcase, Gillis just putting some of his old shirts in. Norma stands staring, speechless, for a second. Gillis moves out of the shot towards the closets.

NORMA
What are you doing, Joe? What are you doing? You're not leaving me?

GILLIS
Yes, I am, Norma.

NORMA
No, you're not.
(Calling)
Max! Max!

GILLIS
Max is a good idea. He can help with my luggage.
(He gestures in the direction of the closet)
Thanks for letting me wear the handsome wardrobe. And thanks for the use of all the trinkets.

He takes the cigarette case and throws it on the chaise longue. Then he throws the lighter, the wrist watch, the platinum key-chain and the tie clip.

GILLIS
(Indicating the bureau)
The rest of the jewelry is in the top drawer.

NORMA
It's yours, Joe. I gave it to you.

11454-52

GILLIS
And I'd take it in a second, Norma -- only it's a little too dressy for sitting behind the copy desk in Dayton, Ohio.

NORMA
These are nothing. You can have anything you want if you'll only stay. What is it you want -- money?

GILLIS
Norma, you'd be throwing it away. I don't qualify for the job, not any more.

NORMA
You can't do this! Max! Max! ... I can't face life without you, and I'm not afraid to die, you know.

GILLIS
That's between you and yourself, Norma.

NORMA
Yoú think I made that up about the gun...

She rushes into her room. Gillis closes the suitcase calmly, notices that he is still wearing some cuff-links Norma gave him, takes them off.

Norma reappears in the door, carrying the revolver.

NORMA
See, you didn't believe me!.. Now I suppose you don't think I have the courage!

GILLIS
Oh, sure -- if it would make a good scene.

NORMA
You don't care, do you? But hundreds of thousands of people will care!

GILLIS
Wake up, Norma. You'd be killing yourself to an empty house. The audience left twenty years ago. Now face it.

7-19-49

During the preceding, Max has entered. He stands listening, paralyzed.

NORMA
That's a lie! They still want me!

GILLIS
No, they don't.

NORMA
What about the studio? What about De Mille?

GILLIS
He was trying to spare your feelings, The studio wanted to rent your car.

NORMA
Wanted what?

GILLIS
De Mille didn't have the heart to tell you. None of us has had the heart.

NORMA
That's a lie! They want me, they want me! I get letters every day!

GILLIS
You tell her, Max. Come on, do her that favor. Tell her there isn't going to be any picture -- there aren't any fan letters, except the ones you write yourself.

NORMA
That isn't true! Max?

MAX
Madame is the greatest star of them all... I will take Mr. Gillis' bags.

He leaves.

NORMA
You heard him. I'm a star!

GILLIS
Norma, grow up. You're a woman of fifty. There's nothing tragic about being fifty -- not unless you try to be twenty-five.

7-19-49

NORMA
I'm the greatest star of them all.

GILLIS
Goodbye, Norma.

NORMA
No one leaves a star. That makes one a star.

Gillis picks up the typewriter and leaves.

NORMA
You're not leaving me!

E-40 STAIRCASE

Gillis descending with the typewriter.

NORMA'S VOICE
Joe! ...Joe!

There is the SOUND OF A SHOT. The glass of the front door is shattered. Gillis at the door opens it and walks out, without looking back.

Down the staircase rushes Norma, a disordered wildness in the way she moves.

NORMA
You're not leaving me!

She hurries after Gillis.

E-41 PATIO (NIGHT)

Dark except for lights from the house and the luminousness of the lit pool.

Gillis is crossing the patio towards the garage. He is carrying the typewriter. He doesn't accelerate his step, although he has heard the shot. Behind him Norma comes from the lighted house.

NORMA
You're not leaving me!

She shoots twice in rapid succession. Gillis drops the typewriter. The shots have swung him around. He is now facing Norma. She shoots him. This shot hits him in the belly. He doubles up, instinctively backs away from her, plummets into the lit pool.

7-19-49

SCENE E-40

11454-277

SCENE E-41

11454-293

SCENE E-41

SCENE E-41

Norma: Stars are ageless, aren't they?

Up the stone steps from the garage rushes Max. He sees the situation, hurries towards Norma, who stands exultant in the strange light from the pool.

NORMA
Stars are ageless, aren't they?

DISSOLVE TO:

E-42 THE PATIO

Dawn is breaking. At the edge of the pool stand policemen, detectives and police photographers. Motorcycle policemen are holding off the mob which is trying to storm the house.

A lietuenant from the Homicide Bureau leaves the crowd around the pool and goes into

E-43 THE LOWER HALL, DESMOND HOUSE

It is filled with a pandemonium of police officers, newspaper people, etc. who are kept from the upper floor by two policemen at the head of the stairs. The lieutenant from the Homicide Bureau goes through the crowd to the telephone at the foot of the stairs, picks up the phone and dials.

LIEUTENANT
Coroner's office? ... I want to speak to the Coroner ... Who's on this phone?

E-44 THE WHITE TELEPHONE IN NORMA'S BEDROOM

Standing talking into it is Hedda Hopper.

MISS HOPPER
I am! Now get off, this is more important ... Times City Desk? Hedda Hopper speaking. I'm talking from the bedroom of Norma Desmond. Don't bother with a rewrite man, take this direct. Ready? -- As day breaks over the murder house, Norma Desmond, famed star of yesteryear, is in a state of complete mental shock ...

THE CAMERA PANS TO ANOTHER PART OF THE BEDROOM, where Norma sits at a mirror, staring at herself blankly. Firing questions at her are the Captain of the Holmby Hills Division and the L.A. Homicide Squad. Max stands by faithfully.

7-19-49

SCENE E-44

Sequence E · 257

SCENE E-44

Head of Homicide: Did you intend to kill him? Just answer me that.

HOLMBY HILLS CAPTAIN
You do not deny having killed this man, Miss Desmond?

HEAD OF HOMICIDE
Did you intend to kill him? Just answer me that.

HOLMBY HILLS CAPTAIN
Was it a sudden quarrel? Had there been any trouble between you before?

HEAD OF HOMICIDE
If it was a quarrel, how come you had the gun right there?

HOLMBY HILLS CAPTAIN
This guy -- where did you meet him for the first time? Where did he come from? Who is he?

HEAD OF HOMICIDE
Did he have a wife? Did he have a girl friend? Did you know them?

HOLMBY HILLS CAPTAIN
Had he been trying to blackmail you?

E-45 PATIO -(DAWN)

The body of Gillis being fished from the pool, put on a stretcher, covered with an army blanket. Two men from the Coroner's office carry it towards the Coroner's hearse, CAMERA PANNING with them.

GILLIS' VOICE
It got to be five in the morning and I was still floating in that pool of hers...Finally they fished me out like a harpooned baby whale. The whole place was jumping by then -- cops, newsmen, columnists, and the usual crowd we get in Los Angeles when they open a super market. Everything but searchlights. Well, they checked the damage, but they didn't have to. I was all set for the Coroner and a nice ride to the morgue,down Sunset Boulevard. Only by then the newsreel guys had arrived, with cameras and celluloid, so I decided to stick around a while. This was too good to miss.

7-19-49

SCENE E-45

SCENE E-45

11454-151

Paramount
News
PARAMOUNT PICTURES INC.
HE EYES AND EARS OF THE WORLD"
11454-160

E-46 NORMA'S BEDROOM

The interrogators are still firing questions at Norma, who sits lifeless, staring at herself. Max watches.

HEAD OF HOMICIDE
Did the deceased ever threaten you? Were you in fear of bodily injury?

HOLMBY HILLS CAPTAIN
Did you hate him? Had you ever thought of doing something like this before?

HEAD OF HOMICIDE
Was theft involved? Did you catch him trying to steal something, or find he had stolen something?

A police lieutenant has entered, goes to the Head of Homicide.

LIEUTENANT
The newsreel guys have arrived with the cameras.

HEAD OF HOMICIDE
Tell them to go fly a kite. This is no time for cameras.

A word has pierced the mists that surround Norma.

NORMA
Cameras? ... What is it, Max?

MAX
The cameras have arrived, Madame.

NORMA
They have? Thank you, Max. Tell Mr. De Mille I will be on the set at once.

Max looks at the Head of Homicide who, after a moment's consideration, nods at him.

MAX
Yes, Madame.

He leaves with the Head of Homicide.

NORMA
(To the others)
You will pardon me, gentlemen. I have to get ready for my scene.

7-19-49

SCENE E-46

Norma: Cameras? What is it, Max?
Max: The cameras have arrived, Madame.
Norma: They have? Thank you, Max.
Tell Mr. DeMille I will be on the set at once.

She takes a comb and runs it through her hair, then starts applying some wild makeup.

E-47 STAIRCASE AND LOWER HALL

Max makes his way down the stairs through the crowd of newsmen to the newsreel cameras, which are being set up in the hall below.

MAX
Is everything set up, gentlemen?
Are the lights ready?

From the stairway comes a murmur. They look up.

Norma has emerged from the bedroom and comes to the head of the stairs. There are golden spangles in her hair and in her hand she carries a golden scarf.

The police clear a path for her to descend. Press cameras flash at her every step.

Max stands at the cameras.

MAX
Is everything set up, gentlemen?

CAMERAMAN
Just about.

The portable lights flare up and illuminate the staircase.

MAX
Are the lights ready?

2ND CAMERAMAN
All set.

MAX
Quiet, everybody! Lights!
Are you ready, Norma?

NORMA
(From the top of the stairs)
What is the scene? Where am I?

MAX
This is the staircase of the palace.

7-19-49

SCENE E-47

NORMA
Oh yes, yes. They're below, waiting for me to dance the Dance of the Seven Veils. I'm ready.

MAX
All right.
(To cameramen)
Camera!
(To Norma)
Action!

Norma arranges the golden scarf about her and proudly descends the staircase. The cameras grind. Everyone watches in awe.

Scene E-47, The Staircase

Wilder in the crane, preparing to shoot Norma's descent down the staircase.

11454-103

11454-14

11454-290

11454-287

above, opposite: Swanson demonstrates to Wilder what she wants to do in her final scene.

11454-2/149

At the foot of the stairs, Norma stops, moved.

NORMA

I can't go on with the scene.
I'm too happy. Do you mind,
Mr. DeMille, if I say a few words?
Thank you. I just want to tell
you how happy I am to be back in
the studio making a picture again.
You don't know how much I've missed
all of you. And I promise you
I'll never desert you again, because
after "Salome" we'll make another
picture, and another and another.
You see, this is my life. It always
will be. There's nothing else -
just us and the cameras and those
wonderful people out there in the
dark... All right, Mr. DeMille,
I'm ready for my closeup.

FADE OUT.

THE END

7-19-49

11454-158

CREDITS

SUNSET BOULEVARD

Directed by Billy Wilder

Written by Charles Brackett, Billy Wilder, and D. M. Marshman Jr.

Produced by Charles Brackett

Music Score by Franz Waxman

Director of Photography ....*John F. Seitz, A.S.C.*
Art Direction ....*Hans Dreier and John Meehan*
Special Photographic Effects ....*Gordon Jennings, A.S.C.*
Process Photography ....*Farciot Edouart, A.S.C.*
Set Decoration ....*Sam Comer and Ray Moyer*
Editorial Supervision ....*Doane Harrison*
Costumes ....*Edith Head*
Edited by ....*Arthur P. Schmidt*
Makeup Supervision.......................*Wally Westmore*
Sound Recording by ....*Harry Lindgren and John Cope*
Assistant Director ....*C. C. Coleman Jr.*

Copyright MCML by Paramount Pictures Corporation

Cast

William Holden ....*Joe Gillis*
Gloria Swanson ....*Norma Desmond*
Erich von Stroheim.........................*Max Von Mayerling*
Nancy Olson ....*Betty Schaefer*
Fred Clark ....*Sheldrake*
Lloyd Gough ....*Morino*
Jack Webb ....*Artie Green*
Franklyn Farnum............................*Undertaker*
Larry Blake ....*1st Finance Man*
Charles Dayton ....*2nd Finance Man*
Cecil B. DeMille.............................*Himself*
Hedda Hopper ....*Herself*
Buster Keaton..................................*Himself (a "waxwork")*
Anna Q. Nilsson.............................*Herself (a "waxwork")*
H. B. Warner..................................*Himself (a "waxwork")*
Ray Evans..*Himself*
Jay Livingston ....*Himself*

1A 50/372 40265

WHEN THE CAMERAS STOP

The cast and crew of *Sunset Boulevard* between takes.

left: Billy Wilder and Charles Brackett visit Gloria at her dressing room during the filming of the New Year's Eve scene.

bottom left: Gloria Swanson in her dressing room, surrounded by flowers from well-wishers.

bottom right: Hedda Hopper in her dressing room.

top: Billy Wilder and Erich von Stroheim ham it up as Nancy Olson (seated) and others look on, during the night shoot at the pool.

above, right: Gloria Swanson shows Buster Keaton the caricature of herself that hangs on the wall between her and William Holden.

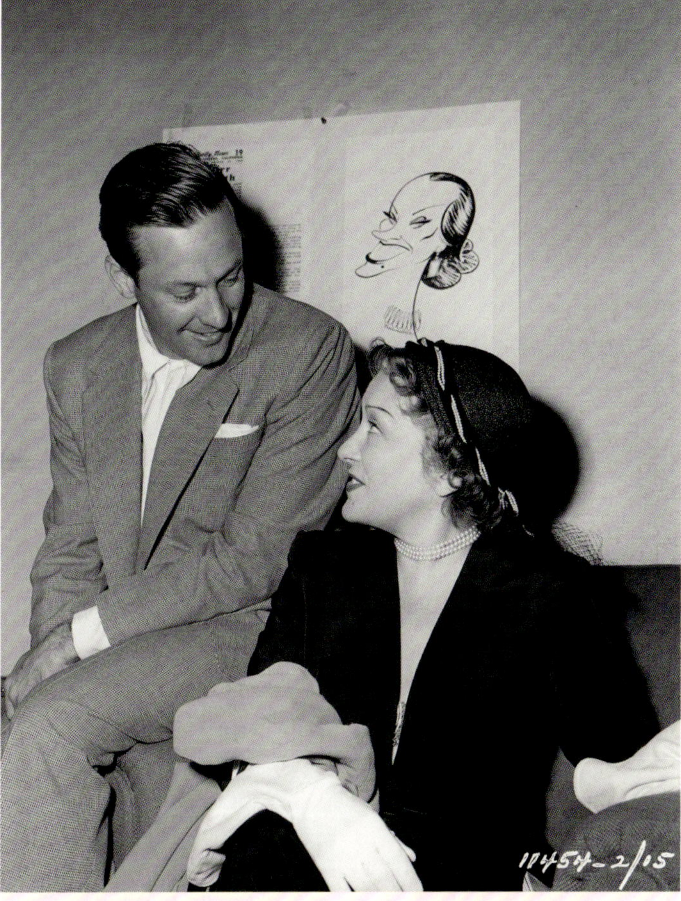

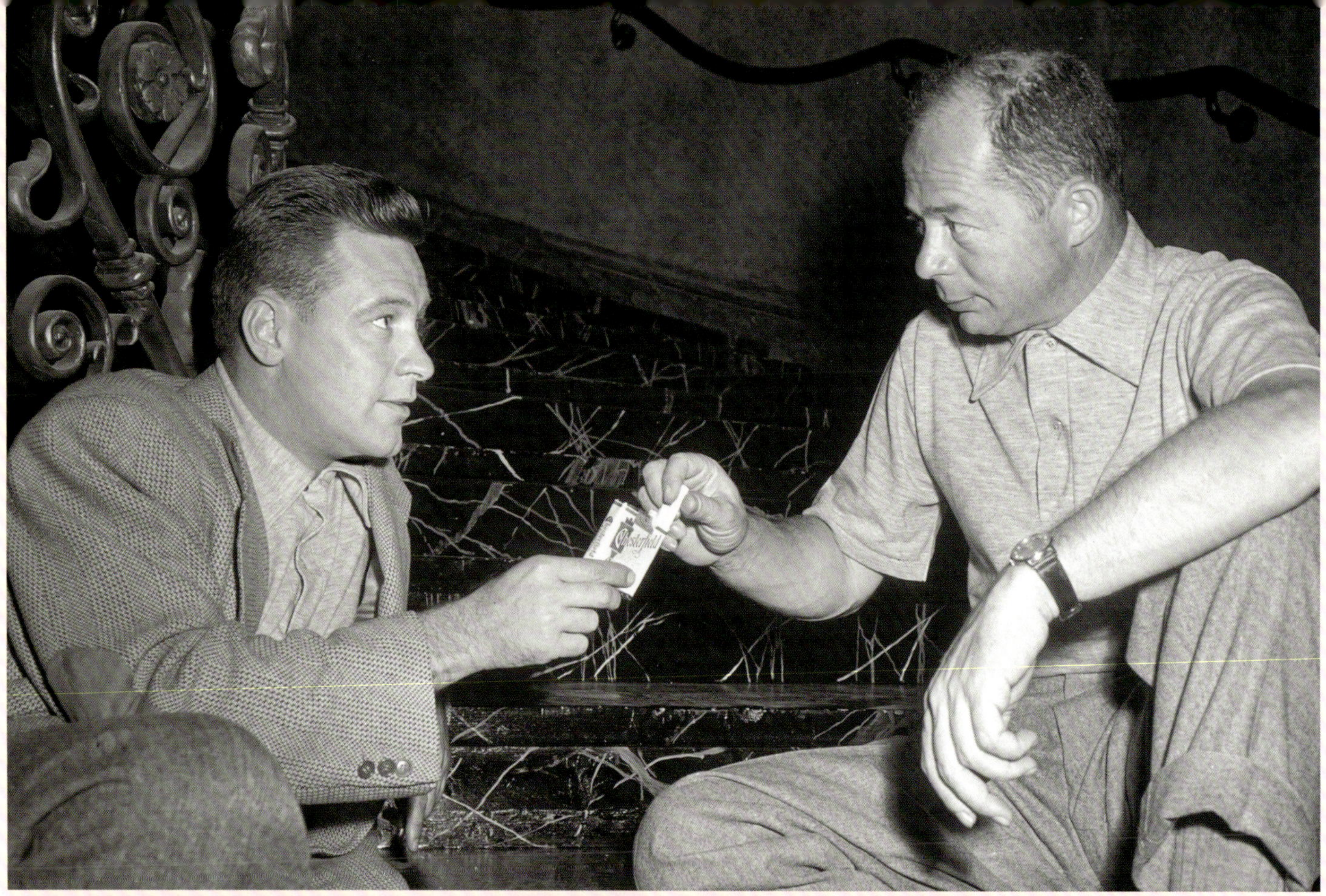

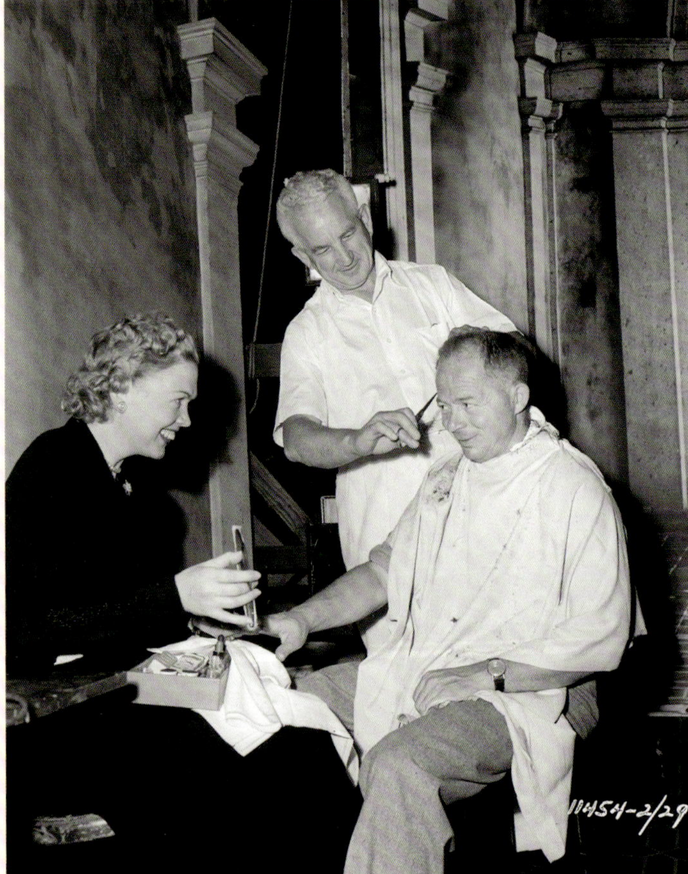

top: William Holden and Billy Wilder take a break on the steps of the mansion.

bottom left: Top directors like DeMille and Wilder had every need catered to by all sorts of in-house services at Paramount. Here, Wilder takes advantage of the barber services.

bottom right: Sidney Skolsky getting touched up for his scene that will ultimately end up on the cutting room floor.

top left: DeMille chatting with actor Henry Wilcoxon, whose working relationship with DeMille goes back to *Cleopatra* (1934).

top right: *Samson and Delilah* extras wait for their call.

left: DeMille, Swanson, and Wilder during rehearsal for the Paramount set scene.

11454-2/9

VISITING THE SET

The *Sunset Boulevard* set was very popular—everyone wanted to stop by to say hello to the stars and watch the magic happen. Here are just a few who did.

opposite: Holden and Swanson between takes of the New Year's Eve scene.

left: Gloria is visited by Edith Head, who designed the costumes for the film. Head considered this film the most challenging of her career. She figured that Swanson would have the best idea of what women would have worn then and would be wearing now, and worked closely with her to develop Norma's look.

bottom left: Paramount star Dorothy Lamour stops by to chat with Gloria.

bottom right: Gloria's daughter Michelle Bridget Farmer visits her mother in her dressing room.

left: Actress Julia Faye catches up with Gloria in her dressing room. The two had worked together in silent films dating back to *Don't Change Your Husband* in 1919.

bottom left: The once King of Comedy, Mack Sennett, reminisces with Gloria about the good old days.

bottom right: Adolph Zukor, one of the founders of Paramount Studios, visits DeMille during the rehearsals for the soundstage scene.

left: Roland Young, on the Paramount lot filming *Let's Dance*, visits Gloria on the bedroom set.

bottom left: Columnist Sidney Skolsky getting a few quotes from Cecil B. DeMille.

below: Ray Milland, the star of two of Billy Wilder's successes, *The Lost Weekend* and *The Major and the Minor*, stops by to chat with Wilder and William Holden on the living room set. Milland was on the Paramount lot filming *Copper Canyon*.

bottom right: Gloria Swanson, Billy Wilder, and Wilder's wife, Audrey Young.

above: William Holden and his wife, Brenda Marshall.
opposite: Cast and crew review a strip of the film with Billy.

ACKNOWLEDGMENTS: My eternal thanks go to Dalton Alfortish, Jon S. Bouker, Manoah Bowman, Paul Lekakis, Allen London, Matthew McCarty, and Megan Vance. Their assistance pulling materials, reading drafts, and finding images for my text was invaluable. —Jeffrey Vance

weldon**owen**

an imprint of Insight Editions
P.O. Box 3088
San Rafael, CA 94912
www.weldonowen.com

CEO Raoul Goff
SVP Group Publisher Jeff McLaughlin
VP Publisher Roger Shaw
VP Creative Chrissy Kwasnik
Executive Editor Karyn Gerhard
Editorial Assistant Jon Ellis
Managing Editor Michelle Hope
Art Director Megan Sinead Bingham
VP Manufacturing Alix Nicholaeff
Production Manager Joshua Smith
Strategic Production Planner Lina s Palma-Temena

Weldon Owen would also like to thank Bob Cooper and Ellen Foreman for their work on this project. Special thanks to Risa Kessler and Sabi Lofgren at Paramount Pictures, and Allison Bermann, Caitlin Denny, Walter Nolasco, Becky Ruud, and Douglas Santos at the the Paramount Pictures Archives; without their tremendous guidance, diligence, and spirit of collaboration this book could not have been made.

ISBN: 979-8-88674-332-6

Manufactured in China by Insight Editions
10 9 8 7 6 5 4 3 2 1

Insight Editions, in association with Roots of Peace, will plant two trees for each tree used in the manufacturing of this book. Roots of Peace is an internationally renowned humanitarian organization dedicated to eradicating land mines worldwide and converting war-torn lands into productive farms and wildlife habitats. Roots of Peace will plant two million fruit and nut trees in Afghanistan and provide farmers there with the skills and support necessary for sustainable land use.

All images courtesy Paramount Studios, with the exception of the following:
Everett Collection: 51, 80, 235; Photofest: 117;
Jeffrey Vance: 10, 12, 13 (both), 14, 15, 20, 176, 284, 287.